Exploring

Other titles by Randell Jones

Scoundrels, Rogues, and Heroes of the Old North State, 2004 & 2007
    by Dr. H.G. Jones, edited by Randell Jones & Caitlin Jones

In the Footsteps of Daniel Boone, 2005
    with *On the Trail of Daniel Boone* (companion DVD), 2005

In the Footsteps of Davy Crockett, 2006 (out of print)

Before They Were Heroes at King's Mountain, 2011

A Guide to the Overmountain Victory National Historic Trail, 2011,
    second edition, 2016

Trailing Daniel Boone, DAR marking Daniel Boone's Trail, 1912-1915,
    2012

The Daniel Boone Wagon Train—a journey through The Sixties, 2013

Interactive, Online Tour of the Overmountain Victory NH Trail, 2014
    (link from www.danielboonefootsteps.com)

Interactive, Online Tour of Daniel Boone's Trail, 2015
    (link from www.danielboonefootsteps.com)

The American Spirit, 1780, 2016 (free YouTube video)
    (link from www.danielboonefootsteps.com)

From Time to Time in North Carolina, 2017

Bearing Up, 2018

Available through Daniel Boone Footsteps
www.danielboonefootsteps.com
1959 N. Peace Haven Rd., #105
Winston-Salem, NC 27106

Exploring

Randell Jones. editor

Daniel Boone Footsteps
Winston-Salem, North Carolina

Life is either a great adventure
or nothing.
- Helen Keller

Preface

This book grew from an interest in helping celebrate in 2019 the 250th anniversary of an important event in American history: Daniel Boone's first passage through the Cumberland Gap into Kentucky in spring 1769. Cumberland Gap is America's first "gateway to the west" and the portal through which a quarter-million immigrants passed from 1775 to 1810 to populate an expanding American frontier.

As part of this celebration effort, we chose to engage modern Americans in writing about experiences in their lives which resonate with themes associated with Boone's experiences during his first excursion into Kentucky, where he hunted for two years. We created the Personal Essay Publishing Project.

We successfully proved the publishing concept in 2018 after launching a pilot project in November 2017. We issued a Call for Essays concerning an event in the life of Daniel Boone in 1767/1768—his wintering over after being trapped by an early snow storm in the mountains of eastern Kentucky. The collection of stories gathered from writers responding to that call on the theme of "making do, bearing up, and overcoming adversity" became **Bearing Up**. That anthology received a Book Award from the North Carolina Society of Historians, who also recognized the project with an Excellence Award.

The book you are holding is the result of our second call for essays issued in summer 2018. The theme is "Exploring: Discoveries. Challenges. Adventure." We thank the several dozen writers in Kentucky, North Carolina, and elsewhere who responded to the Call for Essays by submitting such interesting, thoughtful, and well-crafted stories.

We recognize the artistry of William Tylee Ranney (1813-1857) who painted "Boone's First View of Kentucky" in 1849. A slightly different painting by William Ranney of the same name and showing two figures in the background positioned differently is owned by the Gilcrease Museum in Tulsa, Oklahoma. We thank Fine Art America (fineartamerica.com) for enabling our use of this image for the cover. Notably, William Ranney, born in Connecticut, lived in Fayetteville, North Carolina, during his early teen years and began his artistry there.

This book and Personal Essay Publishing Project are undertaken by author and publisher Randell Jones, doing business as Daniel Boone Footsteps in Winston-Salem, North Carolina.

Thank you for enjoying and appreciating good storytelling. •

RJ

Contents

EXPLORING

Contents

EXPLORING

Contents

xiii

Introduction

E verybody loves a good story; and, everybody has a story to tell. Some folks just need the right opportunity and perhaps a little encouragement to share a tale they want to tell. That is the mission of the Personal Essay Publishing Project, a chance for both new and experienced writers to craft a story from their own lives and then to see their creative efforts around a common theme shared in print in a collective anthology.

The project was born out of a sincere desire to help modern Americans connect with the stories of those who came before us, those who helped create the America of which we find ourselves its current stewards. History is not often a happy story, but our collective history is rich with experiences from which we can learn how best to live our lives into our collective future.

Daniel Boone

One of the icons of America's early years is Daniel Boone. He is America's pioneer hero whose remarkable life spanned 86 years from colonial times before the American Revolution into the rise of Andrew Jackson. During his life, Boone's footsteps passed through what today is divided into 11 states, spanning from Pennsylvania to Missouri, and from the Great Lakes to Florida swamps. (See *In the Footsteps of Daniel Boone* by Randell Jones.)

This year, 2019, is the 250th anniversary of Daniel Boone's first excursion through the Cumberland Gap into Kentucky in spring 1769. He hunted there for two years ranging across the vast interior of what would become the Bluegrass State before returning home to the upper Yadkin River valley of North Carolina. Six years later, he would mark Boone Trace in March 1775 along which some of the earliest immigrants into Kentucky would pass during the following 20 years. Thus, began America's Westward Movement and the unfolding of a history and stories which captive us still today.

Crossing into Ken-te-ke

On May 1, 1769, Daniel Boone left his home on the banks of the Upper Yadkin River in North Carolina and made his way west with a party of five other hunters on the rumor of being able to find a gap through the Appalachian Mountains into Ken-te-ke, the fabled land rich with deer, elk, bison, otter, and beaver. Within the month, Boone passed through the Cumberland Gap for the first time and by June 7 saw from an overlook atop Pilot Knob his first view of the "beautiful level of Kentucky." By summer, the men established a base camp and began to hunt for deer, whose skins would bring a good price back in Salisbury, North Carolina. To help pass the time, Daniel had brought the first book into Kentucky, *Gulliver's Travels*, which he read around the campfire at night to his hunting companions.

The men were having great success with their hunting for the first seven months. In late December, their trespassing was discovered by a party of Shawnee hunters who captured Boone and his brother-in-law, John Stuart. The Shawnees confiscated the hides the hunters had collected by then. After being forced to walk as prisoners for a week, Boone and Stuart escaped only to discover upon their return to their camp that their hunting companions had abandoned them to return east.

Boone and Stuart spent that winter trapping for pelts on opposite sides of the Kentucky River. When Stuart failed to meet at their appointed rendezvous, Boone crossed the river to search for Stuart, discovering his camp but not finding his companion, that disappearance a mystery only solved five years later by happenstance. Boone remained in Kentucky on his own for the next year roaming broadly, scouting the land, and learning the secrets of Ken-te-ke.

Boone returned to North Carolina after two years away with some fascinating stories to tell. Through threatening encounters, discouraging hardships, and surprising discoveries, Daniel Boone explored this new world across the Appalachian Mountains. His stories of all his adventures there emboldened many others to follow in his footsteps. Many did so in the next few years and tens of thousands more poured through the Cumberland Gap during the decades following the American Revolution, following his Boone Trace. Meanwhile, America was busy creating and telling its own story, too—our story.

Telling One's Own Story
To enable writers to connect with the spirit of Daniel Boone

undertaking this exploration of Ken-te-ke in 1769, we issued a Call for Essays during the summer of 2018. In the spirit of exploring, we invited writers to craft a personal story about some experience of their own lives through which they faced a challenge and perhaps discovered something about themselves or through some circumstances experienced what they ended up calling an adventure. Or perhaps their experience was not so positive. In all cases, we invited writers to share their tale in 750-800 words in a personal story. We especially encouraged North Carolina and Kentucky writers to participate.

Exploring

We are gratified by the response to our Call for Essays, and we are grateful to all who invested time and energy into crafting personal stories for possible inclusion in this anthology. We chose essays to include based on the quality of the writing and the resonance of the personal experiences shared with the theme of the call: "Exploring—Discoveries. Challenges. Adventure."

The stories presented here are a testament that good story-telling is alive and well. Some will make you wince, some laugh out loud, and some drift into your own recollections to ponder the experience. All are shared in the hope that your own stories of discovery and adventure during challenging times will come to your mind and that you might write them and share them in your own circles of friends and family.

Everybody loves a good story. Enjoy these. •

A Walk in the Park
by Kyle Paterson

After completing the drudgery of high school, I wanted to forget my run-of-the-mill life in North Carolina and go see the world. I knew life offered more than classrooms and weekend drinking, so, instead of college, I diverged from my peers and signed up for a gap-year program in Patagonia, Chile, to live in the wilderness for six months. I would be backpacking, sea kayaking, and rock climbing in a part of the world about which I knew nothing. My parents were skeptical about my decision. They knew I had no camping experience, lacked fluency in Spanish, and would be immensely far from them. Fortunate for me, they were onboard.

In the United States, we enjoy relative comfort. If it's cold outside, we stay inside; if we get wet, we change clothes; if we're tired, we rest; if we're hungry, we eat. These creature comforts were distant memories when living in the wilderness. If we got tired, we got stronger; if we got wet, we stayed wet; if we were cold, we'd have to get our blood pumping; if we were hungry, we had to wait for our rationed food. This experience was nothing like the life I knew back home, and I loved it.

We lived in small tents, in Patagonia, which is known as being one of the windiest places on earth. Being the southern tip of South America, Patagonia is a small stretch of land separating the cold Pacific air from the warmer air of the southern Atlantic. The change in pressure over such a small area produces dramatically strong winds; and, our living a stone's throw from the Southern Patagonian Ice Field only amplified the effects. For our tents to stay grounded, we tied them down at 12 points to either trees or enormous boulders. It was almost routine for us to leave the comfort of our sleeping bags to go outside and retie our tents because of the wind offsetting our boulders.

I recall vividly my first experience of hypothermia. Our group of 13 was tasked to find a point of access to a nearby glacier in the hopes of crossing it later that week. We crossed three glacial rivers early in our hike that day, soaking our boots and pants. As we climbed a slope of loose rock, rain began to fall, and I had left my rain gear back at camp. As we continued to ascend, that rain turned into snow and that snow turned sideways. After several hours of hiking, conditions began to deteriorate further, so we decided to turn around. During the chilling descent, I lost all feeling in my hands. I gripped onto my trekking poles as hard as I could to keep as much blood flowing as possible. As we crossed back over those three glacial rivers, I knew what cold felt like. My thoughts were numb and simple. I wasn't concerned with anything other than getting warm again, and my fatigued mind knew it would still be some time before that could happen. After arriving at camp, we had to warm ourselves immediately. I wanted to help in making soup and bringing out dry layers of clothing for others, but

I couldn't even move my wrists. I had to use my teeth to open my tent.

Despite the adversity, I never regretted my decision to take a gap year. There was never a moment in the bitter cold that made me want to trade the tranquility of the wilderness for the comfort of an ordinary day back at home. Even at the most demanding moments, I found myself smiling at my spectacularly beautiful surroundings, at the people I was with, and at myself for pushing beyond limits I had unknowingly placed upon myself.

This experience in Patagonia has led me to live an adventurous lifestyle since. Just two months after arriving home from Patagonia, I left for Alaska to work as a commercial salmon fisherman for the summer before college. I have since used the money made there to aid in travelling to Africa, where I climbed Mount Kilimanjaro, and in funding a backpacking trip through Europe. I have gained more than memories from these few adventures. I have gained a new outlook on what life can be. These moments I have experienced at the edges of the world are not just pictures hung upon the walls of my memory but moments that saturate into every pore of my being. These memories, these experiences, these lessons will live always, will teach me continually, and will keep adventure in my heart. •

Kyle Paterson is from Greensboro North Carolina and is currently attending North Carolina State University. He plans to set himself

A Walk in the Park

3

for more adventurous activities after graduation. Kyle has never considered writing publicly before but when presented this project by his mother he felt truly attached to the theme and the stories behind it.

Packable Pieces: Fear and Hope
by Lisa Miracle Ballard

I pull the box from the back of the cupboard. "Granny's button box!" I shout with excitement to no one there. Who cares? I'm tired and dusty and wish I could just snap my fingers to get this house all packed up.

This is a welcome discovery! But for just a moment, I'm not sure I want to look. The cool metal of the box distracts me, I in my reverie. I feel the raised design and rub my fingers across the diamond stamping. I am entranced by its age whispering to me through faded colors. Memories of it swallow me entirely. I close my eyes and drift.

I am running barefoot across braided rugs and wooden floors. I hear voices and laughter, even smelling the baking bread, and for a split second I am right there in her kitchen. Happy. . . .

Jolted awake by the noise of some stack of something falling to the floor, I grab my balance. A disheveled kitchen and the disarray of empty boxes everywhere, shoves reality into my face. Moving. God, have mercy. And send help if you're listening! (Please. I said "please.")

I'm deconstructing, tearing down my life into packable pieces. What to save, what to move, what to let go? Hard choices. This move is like an anvil on my chest. Sometimes I can't breathe. It's the "what-to-let-go" part that's killing me. My suffocations are always about the letting-go part.

Overcoming my earlier hesitation, I pry open the lid. I draw in a sharp breath. How had I forgotten this? Granny's button box. Full of . . . "What is all this stuff?" I ask my dog, who I have learned over the years is quite the good listener. "There's buttons – wow!" I continue. "Old buttons! Old button cards, thread, hooks, eyes, old coins!" (I admit I was easily distracted and surprisingly amused during this tedious packing.) But really now, these buttons and things seem to be arranged in several layers.

Like excavating an ancient ruin, I peel back time, pulling layer after layer out of the box and finding treasures long forgotten. A silk box that once held handmade earrings from Japan is now full of coins. The button card from my great grandfathers' general store—its missing buttons were sewn onto my daughter's christening gown 20-some years ago. I can see my grandmother's hands sewing those little buttons as if she were in front of me now. Skeleton keys to the old home-place. A ring. Whose was this? A tiny little note scrawled out in pencil. A love note to "Mommy" from my daughter when she first learned to make letters. Deeper and deeper into the box I pull out treasure after treasure of days gone by, lives gone on, and only dear memories remaining.

The further I dig into the box the more my heart fills with

anxiety and sadness. I am walking through time – gliding, strolling, remembering. It hurts. My memory muscles ache. This is an excavation of the past, not through dirt or earth but through buttons and notes and tiny boxes covered in Japanese silk. It is an exploration and a visit with my past clashing into my future, confronting me as I prepare for a major move to care for my aging parents—the move I never wanted to make, the move that has turned my life upside down, the move that may be my last. I feel as if I am standing at the interface of time itself, one foot in my past and one foot teetering over my days yet to be written awaiting my decision of where to step and when. I realize in this single instant of time that I am perched across the chasm of the present—a present in which I am not fully living. There it is. I've said it. Ouch!

Big memories and bigger moments spring from this little box. Like a genie out of a bottle, surprise and remembrance emerge and a little bit of fear and hope for the future drift up, too. Yesterday's moments of love, laughter, and calamity anchor me. Generations blend and merge in my hands as I sift buttons and strings and beautiful things gathered by three generations packed away into this box on a whim—just to create this moment of discovery for me. "That's the thing about going on a dig," I explain to my dog. "We are looking for the past and yet it somehow connects us to ourselves and points us to our future."

I am just trying to pack. But today, I've become an archaeologist, digging up bones of a different sort and packing up memories from which another generation might also find hope for its future. •

Packable Pieces: Fear and Hope

Lisa Miracle Ballard lives in Huntersville, North Carolina. An active volunteer and advocate in her community, her heritage inspires her writing which has been shared in community publications, newspapers, schools and churches. She is currently working on a collection of essays, poetry, and short stories reflecting her Appalachian roots. Her story, "The Gift," appeared in the 2018 Personal Essay Publishing Project anthology *Bearing Up*..

Naked in New York
by Nancy Tilly

I met my UNC creative writing professor Max Steele in
New York in 1956, and he introduced me to his friend
David, scion to one of New York's prominent families.
I was impressed. The New York social scene was new territory.
Now, Max called to ask if I'd like to go to David's birthday
party. "It'll be an adventure, Nancy Mac." Wow. I would be
hobnobbing with the jet set.

A friend of theirs, Bob, picked me up.
"Where's Max?" I asked.
"Oh, Max," Bob said. "He's gone home." That was Chapel
Hill. North Carolina.

Here I was, going to the fanciest party ever, and I didn't know
a soul. Bob wasn't easy either. He was part of Max's expatriate
group who'd lived in Paris and been analyzed and who lived
for Art. Only now Bob was a dentist.

We turned into a narrow drive that wound around a wooded
mountain. The house was ancient and intimidating, and filled
with the glamorous, sophisticated people I'd longed to meet.

The terrace gave a perfect view of a lake—the lake the Rockefellers used—in the crater below. The moon rode high in a cloudless sky and spread its glow over the whole place. It was the most romantic scene I could imagine, and I could only think of how I longed to hear an Atlanta accent.

Everyone wore black, which showed how they missed the point of a party. My lavender sheath was the lone dot of color. Waiters passed platters of champagne in silver goblets. Now, champagne I adored. "At home," I said loftily, "we use the silver goblets for water."

Everything I said came out wrong. Luckily most of these people weren't sober enough to notice my *faux pas*. I was the youngest one there and the only Southerner.

Over the mantel hung an abstract scribble by some famous artist, Picasso or Rouault, that a child could have painted. That wasn't the worst of it. These people were speaking French. And here came David and his girlfriend Rachel. Thank God.

"Everybody's speaking a foreign language," I complained, I hoped ironically.

Rachel shot David a knowing glance. "We like to practice our French when we can," she explained, as if to a child. She took my arm. "There's David's mother." She shepherded me over and introduced us.

"How do you do?" I said, in my best Atlanta debutante manner. "Your house is beautiful. I love the way you've decorated it."

David's mother looked me over from amethyst earrings to white high heels. "So nice of you to come," she said, turning her back to find someone more important.

A spurt of fury struck me like lightning, but I had no recourse. Before long I found myself sitting with an enormous porcelain plate of steak in my lap. Bob appeared beside me. Where the hell have you been, I wanted to say, but he was my ride home.

"Oh, hi," I said. "Long time no see."
"Well, yeah," he said. "I haven't seen these people in a long time." He sounded apologetic. "We were in Paris together, you know." As if I didn't.

We'd just finished dinner and dessert when a guy burst in the front door, yelling, "David's taken the Jeep to the Lake!"

"Let's go!"

With me on someone's lap in the front seat, arms and legs sticking out of windows like the Revenooers in Snuffy Smith cartoons, Bob's car bounced down the winding rocky road to the lake. The moon was so bright we could see our shadows, the dock, the boats, a couple swimming to an island. It was like something out of *A Midsummer Night's Dream*.

David splashed out of the water toward us like a sea-creature. He was stark naked. Rachel was suddenly beside me. "Ooh, David," a girl screamed and ripped off her clothes. I mean, stripped naked. Bare. Down to nothing. Bosoms and everything showing. In less than a second, the rest were doing it too.

Naked in New York

11

Bob dropped his clothes without a thought. "C'mon," he said, without looking me in the eye.

I sat on a boulder. "This is certainly not the way we do things in the South."

"C'mon, Nancy," said David. He was standing right beside Rachel and me. The Atlanta code had no nudity protocol.

"Wouldn't you like to go in too?" Rachel asked. I could tell she wanted to.

"No," I said, and wished I were that free. If I joined these normal people, the weight of ten generations of Southern guilt would be mine forever.

"In the South," I said, "a lady keeps her clothes on." Better they should blame my Southern belle-ery than see how stunted I really felt.

I yearned for adventure, to explore new places. But tonight was not my night. •

Nancy Tilly's early years in deep South Atlanta received welcome corrections from the University of North Carolina and a ten-year exile in Chicago where she taught college kids. Marriage to Eben Tilly took her back to Chapel Hill and a writing life. Her novel *Golden Girl*, from FSG, won a prize. Tilly's memoir *Rebel Belle: The Making of a Narcissist* is available on Amazon. She retired to Colorado and is working on a juvenile novel, *The Island Summer*.

The Making of an American
by Doug Cantrell

Opportunity is the American dream.

Martin Himler was born into an Orthodox Jewish family and raised in Hungary in humble circumstances. At 16, his romantic interests were toward a young woman from an upper-class, gentile family. Her family refused him, however, because of Himler's poverty and religion. Unemployed and still distraught over his lost love, Himler defied his family in 1907 and migrated to the United States to make a new life at 18.

Himler arrived in New York City with less than a dollar, expecting a cousin to meet him at Ellis Island. When the cousin failed to appear, Himler, who did not speak English, faced a desperate search for employment, housing, and food. Venturing into a saloon where free food was offered, Himler met a labor agent hiring workers for a coal mine at Thacker, West Virginia. With several companions, Himler was placed aboard a train bound for the mines. A small man, Himler found life as a coal loader difficult. The company agent also withheld his pay, charging him for the train ride, lodging, food, and mining equipment. Himler and his companions escaped the debt peonage of the Thacker operation, walking north into Ohio. He worked there on a street-paving crew. For the next several years, Himler moved from place to place, working at various jobs—washing windows in a hotel, working at another mine in Pennsylvania, at a steel mill in Ohio, and digging the McAdoo Tunnel in New York. Eventually, Himler found employment with a shoemaker in New York who he persuaded to sell factory-made shoes at a larger profit. Both Himler and the shoemaker made good money from this venture before Himler took employment with a merchant house supplying peddlers with goods they sold throughout the United States. Himler quit this job and working as a pack peddler focused on selling to Hungarian miners throughout Pennsylvania, West Virginia, Virginia, and Kentucky. He earned a small fortune pioneering a new method of merchandizing—allowing immigrants to pay for goods after receiving them rather than demanding payment up front as most peddlers required.

Himler then decided to publish a Hungarian-language newspaper for coal miners. Publishers of other Hungarian papers laughed at Himler, predicting an early demise for *Magyar Banyaszlap* (Hungarian *Miners' Journal*). To their chagrin, within a few months, the *Miners' Journal* became the largest circulating Hungarian-language publication in the United States. This venture launched Himler on a successful publishing career.

Not content with living as a successful publisher in New York City, Himler decided to combat prejudice against Hungarian immigrants by establishing an experimental capitalistic coal community in Eastern Kentucky, called "Himlerville." To raise funds, Himler sold stock only to Hungarian miners. All employees of the Himler Coal Company owned stock in the company and in addition to wages received dividend payments when the company was profitable. Unfortunately, the company did not survive the coal slump of the 1920s and was sold at auction in 1927. Himler and most of the Hungarian workers left Eastern Kentucky. Himler settled in Columbus, Ohio, for a time and published *Magyar Banyaszlap* there before moving the paper to Detroit, Michigan. It barely survived the Great Depression.

After the attack on Pearl Harbor in 1941, Himler risked his life and fortune by volunteering for military service. He endured the rigors of boot camp at the age of 55 because he wanted to repay the United States for the economic opportunity the country had provided him. Himler was assigned to the Office of Strategic Services (OSS), the predecessor of the CIA. Colonel Himler directed relief efforts to parts of North Africa and Italy. After the war, his most important job was identifying, arresting, and interrogating Hungarian war criminals. Ironically, Himler, a former Hungarian Jew, decided which Hungarian Nazis would face trial for war crimes. Many of the same criminals Himler interrogated had a hand in remanding his siblings to the Nazi death camps. Himler maintained he took no personal pleasure in the job.

While interrogating Nazi criminals, Himler was visited by the woman he had fallen in love with as a teenager. She asked for help locating her husband, a missing Hungarian army officer. Himler discovered that her husband had been killed in combat.

After his discharge from the OSS, Himler moved to Los Angeles, California, where he wrote as a free-lance journalist until his death in 1961. Himler was an ardent foe of Communism during the Cold War. He knew Communism would destroy the opportunity capitalism afforded America's citizens to succeed. Martin Himler was grateful for the opportunity the United States had given him and millions of other immigrants to overcome the caste system and prejudice of Europe and to make of themselves in America what their drive, ambition, and abilities allowed.

Martin Himler made himself American. •

Doug Cantrell is Professor of History and Department Coordinator at Elizabethtown Community and Technical College in Elizabethtown, Kentucky where he has taught since 1987. He is the foremost expert on the topic of immigrants to the Appalachian coal fields and has written and spoken extensively on the topic. Professor Cantrell has authored, co-authored, or edited 13 books. His two latest are *Belles, Bourbon, Bluegrass and Black Gold* and *The Making of an American.*

Speech Therapy
by Steve Cushman

The speech therapist's name was Laura or Lisa, something that started with an L. My son, Trevor, was three and recently diagnosed with autism. This was our fourth visit. The first few she'd spent testing him. She'd show him a picture of a car or banana or house and Trevor would have to identify these everyday objects.

But on this particular visit, she wanted to work on a specific skill: learning to say *I Want*. She said for autistic children it was hard to understand they needed to say phrases like *I want*, some connection with the way their brain works. I didn't care how the brain worked. I was paying her $75/hour to fix my son.

She held out a piece of bubble gum. Trevor reached for it. *No,* she said, *say I want gum*. He reached again and again, but each time she pulled it back and said, *say I want gum*. He'd say gum and he'd say I want, but he wouldn't say I want gum .

The room was small and white, really no bigger than a cubicle with a door and four walls. There was a metal filing cabinet in one corner, from which she pulled out different papers and assignments and games and on the opposite wall was her small wooden desk. Above the desk a bookshelf filled with titles like *Mono-Syllabic Cures, Taking Control,* and *Dyslexia Is Not a Death Sentence.*

I tell you this because instead of watching what was happening between the therapist and Trevor I looked all around the room, searching for something, anything, to focus on instead of his inability to do this seemingly easy task.

With each of her *Trevor, say I want* requests her voice was growing strained. She was tired of this exercise and of him. He didn't seem to care as he threw a yellow Lego brick at the wall, waited for it to fall to the green carpet and then picked it up and threw it again.

She reached over and grabbed the Lego. He yelled, *give, give,* and she said *Trevor say, I want Lego, say it.* And he didn't, wouldn't, couldn't. You could see it in his eyes, the lack of comprehension. Still, she pushed and pushed.

Now, I'm not a violent man and have never struck a woman, but I wanted to wrap my hands around her neck until she could no longer utter her orders at my son. Instead of strangling her, I excused myself and went to the restroom, closed the door on the single stall in the men's room and cried. Everything Julie and I had felt in the last year, from the knowing something was wrong to denying there was anything wrong to getting Trevor tested and now this woman was torturing him. It was simply too much is what I'm trying to say, so I cried harder than I have before or since.

The therapist didn't smile when I returned, didn't give any false hope of progress, and if she could tell I had been crying she gave no clue. All she said was, *we'll keep working.*

If this were a certain kind of story, I would tell you on the drive home, Trevor said, *Dad, I want to go to McDonald's* or *Dad, I want a toy truck.* But instead, we drove home as we did in those days with me talking and Trevor staring out the window.

Eventually, months later, he did finally say, *I want*, but by then that therapist I hated so much had moved on and Trevor was seeing someone else, Karl, in the long list of therapists we've worked with.

If I could see that therapist, I would tell her thank you. She had a job to do, and she did it. Of course, I didn't really hate her. I hated this thing, autism, and I wanted to take it into a dark room and beat it to death with my hands, with a hammer, with anything I could. But I couldn't and still can't.

Instead, what I can offer parents of recently diagnosed children is the knowledge, the hope, that your children will improve, slowly and surely into the person they are meant to be. That's all I can give you. I hope it's enough.

Trevor is fifteen now. He still "has" autism, is still in various therapies, but it's only a small part of who he is. He's funny and kind, a good kid. Last night when I asked him what he wanted for dinner, he said *I want spaghetti with cookie crumbs.* I didn't know whether to laugh or to cry. And yes, he got what he wanted. •

Speech Therapy

Steve Cushman earned an MFA from UNC-Greensboro and has published three novels, including the Novello-Award winning *Portisville*. Steve's first collection of poems, *How Birds Fly*, is the winner of the 2018 Lena Shull prize. Steve lives in Greensboro, North Carolina, with his family and can be found online at www.stevecushman.net.

Betrayal

by Susan Wilson

S he brought a potted plant. Not a trailing heartleaf philodendron that would grow and subsist whether I granted it attention or not. Drooping and curling, telling me it needed water but still carrying on and eventually turning green leaves to yellow to let me know I had forgotten, and even then trying not to be too much of a bother. A plant that wasn't needy, that knew I had other matters more pressing, a plant willing and able to take a back seat. No. She brought a mum, a cheery white pom-pom that would require care and feeding and eventual planting for a chance at survival. A plant that would ultimately drop its pointed petals on the table, leave a mess for me to clean, and then shrivel into a dark, black, spindly skeleton. A plant that would offer me little but require so much.

We met more than 20 years ago. She was an overworked department head, putting in too many hours, looking for part-time help. With three young children, two dogs, and one husband, a part-time job was just what I wanted. We had attended the same university and completed the same major. A perfect match for her analytical mind; a compromise for my creative, less lucrative first choice. We found ourselves to be alike in other ways: sharing a love for Labrador Retrievers, growing up on a farm, preferring salads without onions. Our work led to lunches with colleagues then dinners and conversations without them.

Though boss and employee, we became more like equals, asking the other's opinion before a potential misstep could lead to an unfortunate stumble. We became experts at politely expressing disagreement with corporate positions, parsing slightly bitchy emails destined to offend into constructive responses dripping with diplomatic disapproval. We became sounding board and springboard, paving the other's way, watching each other's back.

I knew before she told me that things weren't quite right. She missed meetings and deadlines. Her wardrobe was different, her conversations clipped short.

"Keep this just between us," she said as she disclosed her unanticipated secret.

Her husband was cheating with a stripper. She'd had no idea he knew of gentlemen's clubs or that he took 3-hour lunches, that he was paying rent on an apartment she'd never seen, allowed someone else to sleep in her bed. Her distress seemed immeasurable. She told me of the day she'd left work early, then met a strange car heading out the dead-end road on which they lived. He'd dismissed the car as someone just lost, a wrong turn taken while looking for somebody else.

"I would have danced naked around the pole in the basement. All he had to do was ask."

She was shattered by his betrayal, feeling responsible for the failure of another. I held her and told her it would be all right. I didn't tell her he would never have asked. He'd already found somebody else.

I kept her secret and dried her tears, did my job and hers. I helped her hide assets while I hid my own; I kept evidence safe, and never let evidence appear. Supportive when she gave him another chance, I never said I told you so when that chance predictably didn't work out. We celebrated when the papers were finally signed, when she went back to being herself, when I went back to being just me.

She rebounded well, finding purpose in the work she'd once abandoned, the work I had learned to do so well, so seamlessly no one noticed it was me. I was happy to see her return, content to continue keeping her secrets. Our work found praise, and she gained a raise and a new office too far away for email deliberations. The rungs on the ladder kept getting higher and higher, challenges she was able to conquer. Our dinners and conversations became fewer and fewer. Unburdened, thriving, and excelling, she is stronger than ever while I still watch her back.

Then my world fell apart, all to pieces, completely.

She stopped by the hospital room on her way to a meeting; time was short, but I'm sure she stayed at least two minutes, perhaps it was closer to three. She told me I was strong and resilient; she was sure we would all be fine, confident I would figure out what to do next … and she brought me a mum. •

Susan Wilson lives in Clemmons, North Carolina, and is a member of Winston-Salem Writers. Her creative nonfiction work has appeared in *Flying South* and *Bearing Up*. She was a finalist for the 2017 James Hurst Prize for fiction and a finalist for the 2018 North Carolina State University Shorter Fiction Prize. She is currently working on a collection of creative nonfiction.

Apprehension and Transcendence

by Valerie Paterson

We landed in a small Chilean airport with only two gates. I sat next to my 19-year-old son on the bus from Balmeceda to Coyhaique, looking at the greening grasses of early spring in the valley and at the snow-capped mountains not far away. It may sound pretty with that bit of description, but it did not feel that way to me. The sprawling valley looked like something out of an old cowboy movie. Shrubs and an occasional tree dotted the hills and rocks. Once in a while we would see a house or a shack. I sat quietly with a knot in my stomach. He sat quietly as well. *What is he thinking? Does he want to turn around and go back home?* We are in the middle of nowhere—at least it seemed that way for us suburbanites of North Carolina.

As we approached the mountain town of Coyhaique we passed a sign: NOLS, National Outdoor Leadership School. That's where Kyle would be starting his adventure into the depths of Patagonia. He wanted to experience something new and differ-ent for his gap year after high school. He had never been camping before—other than in our backyard. He didn't know exactly what he was in for, but *that was* the exploration. His ultimate 6-month, camping adventure with mountaineering, mountain climbing, ice trekking, sea kayaking, and rock climbing awaited.

In making his gap year decision, traveling 5,000 miles from home, living in the wilderness of Patagonia, having no contact—yes, *no contact*—with anyone other than the group he was with—sounded far more appealing than classroom learning at the colleges where he was accepted. The descriptions on the website were intriguing, and we talked to NOLS graduates, who made no pretentions about this being a walk in the park.

In supporting Kyle's choice, apprehension stepped in. Mine, not his. *Isn't he worried about going away for so long, sleeping in a tent on the ground every night? Who wouldn't be? At least what normal person wouldn't?* I trusted that Kyle was fine with his decision, but I still couldn't bring myself to send him off on multiple planes and busses alone. So, my husband and I took this opportunity to experience Patagonia for ourselves … but staying in hotels.

In preparation, I did my best to be sure Kyle had gaiters, gloves, glacier glasses, spork, bowl, head gear, footwear, and all the moisture wicking, insulated, non-insulated, convertible, waterproof, windproof, lightweight, heavyweight, medium weight layers of clothing necessary for surviving in Patagonia. I stayed up half the night worrying before Kyle was to meet his group. What if he got Montezuma's revenge? A cold? A headache? Blisters? Sunburn? A crick in his neck from sleeping on the ground? I was an emotional disaster by the time Kyle woke up to meet his group. Here I was sending my youngest child off and I wouldn't be able to talk to him or know how he was doing for months. I cried and cried and cried that morning. And then I simply had faith in Kyle—my son—and what he had decided.

It took me only a few hours to transform my tears and feelings of loss into wonder and amazement at this magnificent land. I hiked up the Osorno Volcano and marveled at the expansive view as I rode back down in the gondola. I left the warmth of the enclosed area on our tour boat to enjoy a pisco sour, standing on the windy bow just yards away from the Gray Glacier. Our picnic with a tablecloth and wine in the spectacular Torres del Paine National Park was complete with a Chilean flicker foraging for insects nearby, an armadillo following me away from the tour group surrounding him, and the vision of Cuernos del Paine above Lake Pehoe. The sound of a house-sized chunk of ice calving from the Perito Moreno Glacier caught everyone's attention as we watched the waves it created cause the floating ice bergs to rise and fall with the ripples.

My first steps into Patagonia were with apprehension. My last were transcendent. Patagonia is a land of rugged terrain and extremes in weather. It's a land to challenge the physical abilities of mere humans and to be transformed and rewarded spiritually if able to do so. My own emotional Patagonia of leaving Kyle so far from home challenged me, but my own experience of the dramatic landscape left me with the peace of mind of knowing that Kyle would be transformed himself. •

Valerie Paterson lives in Greensboro, North Carolina, and is a member of NC Writers' Network. She is writing a memoir of her experiences as shared in "Me Alone," published in *Bearing Up*. She is an award-winning quilt maker. Her work has appeared in *Free-Motion Mastery in a Month: A Block a Day to Machine Quilting Success* by RaNae Merrill. She and her husband love to dance the Argentine Tango.

EXPLORING

Silence of Sheep Mountain

by Patricia C. Everett

When I first arrived at Sheep Mountain, a table-top mesa in the South Dakota Badlands, my heart swelled at the view. A 360-degree vista painted green, red, orange, and yellow ran to every horizon where a blue umbrella sky rolled back onto me. I had a few moments of absolute silence, the sort filled with a comforting peace that lets you know that only here and now matters. It was nothing like the city I had left behind where one noise cancels out another until there is nothing but muted chaos. So, I held onto this new silence as long as I could.

Back home in the big city, I told many people about it. Several stopped me before I could finish to tell me where they first experienced the same total silence. Each face softened into the same peace even though each spoke of a different place: Nepal, the Serengeti, and even a Pennsylvania farm.

When I told a long-time friend, she said, "So, you are getting it." Although she didn't say it, I heard her thought, *Finally*.

Through the summer and fall, I practiced this silence while

anxiety swirled around me. I am glad I did, because by the end of the year I needed that calm silence in my heart. My father had a stroke the day after Christmas; he was placed on a respirator. I, of course, was filled with all the dread that comes with that phone call—and with the agonizing decisions my family would have to make.

My father and I have had long silences between us. They always started with a slamming door—first the one to my bedroom, then the one to whatever car I owned at the time. But now, I had to face the silence with my father in a way I never had before. Before I went home to see him, I called my friend. We talked a long time. She ended our conversation with a recollection, "Remember that place in South Dakota." She meant Sheep Mountain.

I did remember it. The first time I went into the ICU room, I could only stay with him for five minutes. As I went to see him again and again during his three-month illness, I could sit next to him and even let him hold my hand for longer and longer. And each time before I went back, my friend would say, "Remember Sheep Mountain."

The turning point with my father came on a weekday in February when my mother was too ill to visit him. I took off from work and drove down to be with him, just in case it was THE day. I did not want him to die alone. I sat with him for an hour, then I went to their house to make Momma soup.

I went to see him every two weeks. I saw him grow thinner and weaker. Because his mind stayed clear, he became more frustrated. I felt no one should have to live this way. I had many angry moments and many crying jags, but when I saw him, I could sit beside him silently—more comfortably each time.

In time, the doctors agreed to follow his wishes to turn off all the machines. We moved him to hospice care. I was there for Momma and for him. My mother, sister, and I took turns at his bedside for the 36 hours he lingered off the machine. Afterward, my aunt and uncle came into town and threw a *bon voyage* party.

When my father moved from the ICU to hospice, he mouthed in a bare whisper, "It is so quiet." The harsh, cranking rhythm of the respirator was gone. It was quiet as I sat beside him on my turn as we looked out through the fifth story window at the blue sky. I thought of the big, blue sky on Sheep Mountain and I was comforted. Then, I remembered that Sheep Mountain was not the first time that I experienced such a sky or such a comfortable peace. I first felt that way out on a raft past the breakers in the Atlantic Ocean in the hot sun, with my father anchoring the rafts for me, my sister, and my cousins as we baked all day. I shared that recollection and then I smiled so that he and I knew that we both heard nothing but the waves lapping up on the rafts.

My father died later that afternoon on my sister's watch. Now, when big-city tensions crash over me, I go in my mind to Sheep Mountain on the Great Plains, releasing my heart into the quiet of the wide-open spaces. •

Silence of Sheep Mountain

Patricia C. Everett lives on Lake Norman in Cornelius, North Carolina. After moving from Washington, D.C., in 2016, she joined the Charlotte Writers Club (CWC). Her first CWC submission, "The Dividing of the Stuff," won the one-time Helen Copeland Short Story Contest. She worked as a newspaper reporter then as a software technical writer, and most recently at the U.S. Forest Service, where she writes guides to ensure fire-fighting heroes have the right data.

Seasoned Hikers

by Kaye Threatt

Having a passion for hiking and the Blue Ridge Parkway, in 2004 my husband, Harold, and I decided we would try to hike all the National Park Service trails along this nearly 500-mile scenic byway. We counted 117 trails on our list. In no particular order, we hiked from Mountain Farm Trail near the northern terminus of the Parkway in Virginia to Water Rock Knob near Cherokee, North Carolina. We detailed each trail in a journal. Harold made notes of the temperatures, the distances and the compass readings while I focused on identifying the flora and the fauna. We became seasoned hikers.

Springtime on the Blue Ridge Parkway has a plethora of surprises. Wildflowers emerge and birdsong fills the air. My eyes scan the woodlands for flame azalea and jewel-toned trillium. This is the time of year we see other hikers; they love God's earth. They recommend books and share knowledge of other trails. Many of the hikers are dog lovers, given the number of canines that we encounter.

Summer brings the blooms of mountain laurel and rhododendron to light up the forest. Blanketing the ground is the unmistakable galax, a plant native to these mountains. It has a wondrous fragrance; I can smell it long before I can see it. Butterflies flutter around, crickets chirp in the meadows and water babbles in the brooks. Crossing a cool stream offers a little respite from the heat. Turtles sunbathe on the stream logs. The true pleasure of a summer hike is to come upon a blackberry patch. The sweetness and the tartness intermingle! Blueberry bushes line the trail, tempting us to stop for a healthy snack. We are acutely aware that some of God's other creatures may also be dining out. Once my husband caught sight of a black bear, but I only heard it lumbering off into the verdant forest.

Autumn is a splendid season for hiking. The deciduous trees are spectacular with their colorful leaves. What could be better than spotting wild turkeys on a November day? We make rustling sounds while tramping through the fallen leaves, causing the gobblers to flee. The meadows are dotted with milkweed and goldenrod, bowing to us as we pass. Not to be missed is the big sky that avails itself when we come to a clearing. On a fortuitous day, a kettle of migrating hawks appears on our radar. We pause and reflect; the days are getting shorter, the nights longer—but the length of each trail remains the same.

Winter on the Blue Ridge Parkway is a wonderland—things look so different. We stop, look around, listen and become gratefully aware of our panoramic surroundings. The only skyscrapers are the tall trees and mountain peaks, the rush-hour traffic is reduced to zero and the sounds of the city are far behind us. We wander and wonder. Every trail has its season.

My favorite Blue Ridge Parkway trail is the popular Bluff Mountain Trail at Doughton Park at Mile Marker 238.5 to 244.7. This iconic park provided some of our fondest memories. We met a park ranger hiking on his day off, accompanied by his girlfriend and adopted puppy, Alle, named for Alleghany County where they rescued her. Then there were the Brits who had flown to Augusta, Georgia, for a week of golfing. Being an adventurous lot, they rented a car and drove north to experience the BRP.

Most memorable of all was the World War II veteran who was traveling the Parkway alone. He was retracing the route he and his recently deceased wife had taken in 1958, one year after they were married. Frank was following Elsie's recently discovered journal from that trip. He had stopped for lunch at Alligator Back Overlook. As we rested on the stone wall, he approached us, sharing his heart-touching story. We later learned Frank had no one else to tell; we became his grateful listeners.

And, of course, it would be unthinkable to mention this section of the Blue Ridge Parkway without saluting the veteran waitresses at the Bluffs Cafe. They were dedicated, some working there from its opening in 1949 until its closure in 2010.

On a crisp October day in 2008 we completed our quest of 117 trails while on Sharp Top Trail at Peaks of Otter, Virginia. We trudged up the mountain, posed for photos and gave each other jubilant high fives. As we began our descent, three wide-

Seasoned Hikers

35

eyed deer crossed the path, walking in single file. We likened it to a parade without fanfare, paying tribute to our feat. Our four-year adventure along the Blue Ridge Parkway has left us with a deep appreciation for this most soulful of national parks. •

Kaye Craddock Threatt lives in Winston-Salem, North Carolina. She taught second grade in Virginia and was employed for 20 years as a primary reading teacher in the Winston-Salem Forsyth County Schools. In that capacity she found many opportunities to teach creative writing. In early retirement, she co-edited the Reynolda House Museum of Art newsletter. She still enjoys finding occasions to write and vows to keep the art of letter-writing alive. Kaye's hobbies include hiking, duplicate bridge, and quilting.

Last Dance

by Elizabeth Solazzo

I live each day as if it were my last because I've learned we
never know when we are having our last dance. Or our
last snuggle with the baby or the last hug from a friend, or
the last embrace with our lover. It is only when looking back
that I am aware my husband and I have danced our last time
together.

I spoke to my little brother the morning before he died in a car
crash that ended his life so soon, but I don't recall what we
said. Probably something trivial about half-baked weekend
plans or what he might have for dinner with his girlfriend.
Most of that week is a blur of suffering that has softened
around the edges of my mind during the past 30 years.

I counseled a young pregnant woman in the days before her
boyfriend murdered her and hid her body in trash bags and
sent it down the Haw River. Her body was found many weeks
later, snagged in the weeds along the riverbank, and I was
shocked to discover her almost empty folder in my file cabinet
many months later. She would never return to school to create

a better life for herself and that of her unborn child as we had discussed, her eyes bright with anticipation as she completed her application in blue ink that smudged the page.

I worked with my closest colleague and mentor in the weeks before he died from a massive stroke one Friday afternoon, his office still filled and waiting for his return. Co-workers packed up items that had graced his office walls for over twenty years. Sorrow filled my heart to watch the departure of his vintage medieval knight in full body armor. The silent soldier I had coined Rusty lived in one corner of his office. I regretted never asking why he had that particular piece and why he brought it to the office. Maybe it represented his quirky nature.

Grandparents left me with childhood memories of a long, fat black snake crawling on a ledge of the old chicken house and warm summer evenings sitting on the front porch swing with them as dusk descended over the hills. The comfort of snuggling into a fluffy, featherbed mattress would live in my heart forever.

I sat alongside my sisters, holding vigil over my lingering mother, praying this would be her last day with half-closed eyes and ragged breath, as she had already suffered through many days of illness and pain. Her physical body had been worn thin for many years, trapping her in a recliner in front of the TV, but her heart soldiered on. I prayed for God to release her from this earthly hold and take her into his heavenly home.

Once I felt desire to end a life for the pain they caused. This vile man had injured beyond reason, regret, or repair.

Practicing restraint enabled me to avoid the harsh reality of a prison cell. I trusted in karma to seek revenge.

Standing on a Hawaiian beach or overlooking the crowds surrounding the Colosseum in Rome, I accepted this would be a once-in-a-lifetime experience. The world is large with too many places to visit. But we never know what tomorrow might bring our way, do we?

My first granddaughter is moving away to college this fall and I miss those sweet sleep-overs from long ago. We always enjoyed extra snuggles before we rose. She raised me so well and I became a wonderful grandmother to those who followed. I am proud of the amazing young woman she is today and take some credit for that. She will always have a special spot in my heart, as I hope I do in hers.

I have come to accept that we must live as if these are our last days—on everything. Because they very well might be. And we don't want to miss them.

I still dance with my husband in his wheelchair, if in a different way than we once did. We love one another in spite of his limitations and my endless caregiving, although in a deeper, different way. Our last times on the clock run out as we wonder what tomorrow might bring. All our moments are special even if we are too busy living life to make note of them.

As we get older there are more last times. We grow to expect it. My mother used to qualify her acceptance of an invitation or a plan, by saying, "If I'm still here." I always asked where she planned to be if not here, trying to reassure her that she would be around. And she was—until she wasn't. •

Elizabeth Solazzo lives in the North Carolina piedmont. She writes about family and relationships, most recently in *Chasing the Wind*, a collection of short stories. Her collection of essays, *Saxapahaw Girl*, is about family connections and coming of age in small-town America. Her forthcoming novel is loosely based on her grandmother, a widow struggling in the hills of Appalachia in the early 20th century. Learn more at elizabethsolazzo.com.

A Storm of Trials:
Learning To Be a Pioneer
by Beth Bixby Davis

The Blizzard of '93 was a bear. It roared in without warning. Not then being connected to instant weather apps, as we are today, we were surprised and dangerously unprepared.

I left work that Friday, March 12, and headed for the grocery store. It was time to re-stock our groceries. After filling my cart, I rolled it to my car as tiny snowflakes gently swirling in the crisp air surprised me. Early signs that winter was over had started to appear, but any hopes that spring was here to stay were soon dashed.

Snow continued throughout the evening. Sometime in the night the wind started howling and the temperature dropped to lows below zero. In the morning, startled at the white-out conditions, my husband and I bundled up, cranked up our 4-wheel-drive truck and intended to head for the barn to take care of our four horses. Having barely started, the truck bogged down in the deep snow in our driveway. It wouldn't budge.

At this point, we realized this was a serious blizzard and we were in trouble. We would have to walk through the woods and fields to reach our barn. We needed more layers of warm clothes; we dug out our ski suits, tall boots, toboggans, scarves and thick insulated gloves.

The drifts were waist high and we'd need to walk through them about a half-mile, the shortest route possible. Never did I comprehend how difficult it could be to wade through deep snow during a blizzard with the chill factor well below zero. With each difficult step, my exhaustion increased. My legs started cramping and I experienced shortness of breath. A strong wind stung our eyes with icy snowflakes and our cheeks became numb. As we struggled forward, we came to realize how someone could die in a blizzard. The thought became terrifying as we wondered if we would survive this. Exhausted, we reached the barn, its roof piled high with snow.

We discovered frozen water pipes and an already fragile barn roof in danger of collapsing from the snow's weight. We knew we had to turn the horses out of their stalls in case the roof caved in. We fed them grain, opened their stall doors and let them out. We also knew we could not make this trip twice a day, which was their normal feeding schedule, so we threw out several bales of hay. Apologetically, I said to the horses, "Guys, you're going to have to eat snow. The water is frozen and there is absolutely nothing I can do to help."

We trudged back to the house. Because we had made something of a path, our return trip was a little easier, but even that trail was quickly filling in with snow. Back in my kitchen,

I decided to make a pot roast from the chuck I had purchased the day before. I browned and seasoned it, put it in a casserole dish, and put it in the oven to slow cook for dinner later. My husband built a fire in our wood stove fireplace insert, our only source of heat.

As the blizzard continued, we watched local news alerts and realized this storm was becoming treacherous. Then our power went out. No lights, no water, and our wood stove would have to be kept very low because the fan on the insert would not work. I removed the casserole dish with the pot roast from the non-working oven and set it on the shelf of the wood stove.

Fortunately, my husband had camping supplies. He found his gas lantern and camp stove. We had plenty of candles and a couple of antique oil lamps. We also had a kerosene heater where we tried to melt snow for flushing water – not an easy task. We slept in a bedroom with east facing windows, figuring it would be warmer in the morning- if the sun ever shone again.

On Sunday morning we awoke to bright sunshine, blindingly reflective off the snow. The blizzard had passed. The smell of the pot roast was wonderful. What a welcome dinner we would have after the cold canned goods and peanut butter sandwiches we had been eating. We still made trips to the barn, still endured no power or water, but that night we would eat well. The later addition of potatoes, carrots and onions to that slow-cooked pot roast made it the most delicious food I had ever put in my mouth. We were grateful.

We survived, plowed out a few days later. We soon heard tragic stories of others less fortunate. That ferocious "Storm of the Century" had stalked us, had tested our abilities to endure unexpected hardship. But we faced those trials like pioneers relying on ourselves and making do with what we had. •

Beth Bixby Davis was born in Northern New York and moved to the Asheville area of North Carolina in the mid-1960's where she reared her family, raised Arabian horses and had a 30-year career in nursing. Enjoying a long-time hobby of writing essays and poetry, she recently has taken classes in flash fiction and poetry writing. She belongs to Talespinners Writers Group.

The Farm Summer
by Susan Proctor

It was 1950 and I was 7 years old the first time I went to spend a summer with my cousins in Newberry, South Carolina. Aunt Margaret, Uncle Eston, and my cousins—Sandra, Doyle, Carl, Howard and Barry—were visiting us in Charlotte. When it came time to leave, Aunt Margaret said, giving me a wink, "Susan, I think we'll just take you home with us."

First the begging, "Please let me go," followed by the you'll-get-there-and-want-to-come-home objections then the no-I-won't- promises. At last, Aunt Margaret said to my mother, "Carol, throw some clothes in a bag for this child and we'll be on our way!" With that, the argument was over.

We piled into the yellow station wagon and pulled onto the road. Stories and road games like "Cow Poker" and "I-Spy" made time fly by. Before I knew it. we were pulling in their driveway.

The yard had not one blade of grass but bore the telling brush marks of Aunt Margaret's broom. A single chinaberry tree adorned the front yard. Its branches were positioned perfectly for climbing and if you carefully split the skin of a berry with your fingernail and held it just so, you could shoot it halfway across the yard.

Barry and I were the same age, so we shared the chore of gathering eggs every morning before breakfast. The first time he showed me how to reach under the hen to grab an egg, as soon as I felt the warmth of it, I flung that egg splat on the ground!

What we loved most was exploring. We caught tadpoles in the creek, played hopscotch in squares drawn in the dirt, and made yards of garlands in a meadow of clover. But we were absolutely forbidden to go in one pasture. That was the domain of Jax, the bull. Right in the center of it stood a magnificent oak tree. And oh, how that tree called us to climb it! Every day we gazed at it, imagining such an adventure. "I bet we could touch the clouds," Barry would say.

One day, as it happens with children, the tree won. Jax was nowhere to be seen, so we scampered over the gate and sprinted toward the tree. Up and up we climbed. As we neared the top, we heard a startling sound—loud snorting. Jax had spotted us. He charged the tree. With hooves pawing the ground, he threw himself against the trunk with more power than we could have imagined. The tree shook; its limbs swayed. We screamed and clung on for dear life. Barry called for Aunt Margaret, "Mama! Maaaaama!"

Aunt Margaret came running out of the house to see what was the commotion. Standing not far off the back porch and drying her hands on a dishcloth, she sized up our predicament. "Well, if this don't beat all, Barry Smith!" Why is it you think you're not allowed in there?" Without waiting for an answer, she made her decision. "A bull can't climb a tree. He'll tire of you soon enough. Just sit tight till your daddy comes home for dinner. Once I get hold of the two of you, you'll wish Jax had got you!" She went back in the house shaking her head.

I started to cry. Uncle Eston won't be home till dinner! She's going to leave us up here all day? I'd forgotten that on the farm, they call lunch "dinner" and our city dinner, they call "supper." Sure enough, we soon heard Uncle Eston's car pull up. The car door slammed and then he was soon standing at the gate. "Well, I see you two have had a busy morning. I've a good mind to go have my dinner and leave you up there." With that said and knowing the mischief of children all too well, he walked Jax to his pen and then called to us, "Alright, get yourselves down and go on in the house. I can't say what trouble awaits you there."

Trouble indeed! Aunt Margaret gave Barry and me a good "what for" and took away our privileges for the rest of the week. But even mad, she never made me feel like I was just some no-account kid and she'd have really been happy if Jax had gotten me. No, I felt different at Aunt Margaret's, like not worried something bad was fixing to happen to me any minute. I liked it – that feeling. I had found me a new normal. You know that song Bonnie Raitt sings, *Angel From Montgomery?*

The Farm Summer

47

It has that sweet, plaintiff lyric – "just give me one thing I can hold on to." I didn't know it then, but that summer gave me something I could hold on to. •

Susan Proctor is a native of Charlotte, North Carolina. During her sales & marketing career, she wrote persuasive copy in both corporate and non-profit arenas, to encourage buying, contributing, and volunteering. An active member of Charlotte Writers Club, she won recognition as a frequent contributor. In addition, her work has appeared in literary journals including Jewish Values On-Line and Lilith magazine. Her story, "My Mensch," appeared in the 2018 Personal Essay Publishing Project *Bearing Up*.

Eye of the Dolphin

by Arlene Mandell

L ittle did I know it, but discovery awaited me—
above and below the water.

I had just moved from New York City to Miami. I was sending
out resumes and waiting to land a new job. I wanted to keep
busy in the meantime, so I checked the local newspaper's
volunteer section. One notice caught my eye immediately. They
were looking for people to work with handicapped artists.
Being an artist myself, I saw that as a promising opportunity.

I went for an interview and met John, the manager. He showed
me around and introduced me to the group of artists, including his son, Rick, severely affected with cerebral palsy. Most of
the artists had limited movement in their limbs and they
needed help with paint tubes and brushes. I stayed for the day
and loved it. I continued coming back.

This was a world way outside my realm, far from my common
experience. In my world, I was free to create in whatever way
I chose, but here were artists painting with their mouths, their

feet, or only through the partial use of their hands. They were down-to-earth souls, accepting of their conditions, eager to get to work.

A fun-loving bunch, too! One mischievous day, when I was away on a break, everyone found a way to throw paint at everyone else, rejoicing in the chaos. Their laughter echoed throughout the facility all afternoon. They were buddies, teasing and helping each other, and interpreting one another's speech for me when I could not understand. They were a family.

After working with these artists for several months, I was invited, if I were a good swimmer, to go along on their annual trip to a dolphin refuge in the Florida Keys. There, with the help of volunteers, these gentle spirits would swim with the dolphins. The local TV station would be there to record the event. I was excited to go!

The whole group first assembled with the instructor for a talk on the habits of dolphins, including a list of serious "do's-and-don'ts": DO NOT reach your hand out if they approach you; DO keep your hands at your sides. I was amazed to learn that dolphins can sense a pregnant woman or an injured person. The dolphins will encircle and protect them.

The volunteers were given fins, goggles, and a snorkeling mask to wear, none of which I had worn before; but, we received a quick lesson on how to use them. All together it was a lot to remember, but I thought I could manage. At the last came a crucial reminder: an extremely handicapped human being is depending on me to keep him alive in the water. My job was to be constantly vigilant as I helped Rick enjoy his day.

A moving platform lowered all of us into the water and I was off with Rick, while his dad stood watching from the rim of the dolphin pen. The fins felt awkward on my feet, but otherwise I thought I had the situation in hand until shortly after we started when the goggles fogged up and it was hard to see.

I remembered being told if that happened, to take them off, spit into the mask and slosh it around in the water, but I could not do that without letting go of Rick. Though I couldn't see very well, I was still able to breathe through the snorkeling tube. However, keeping the snorkel and Rick above the water while propelling us around was now becoming more difficult with the clumsy fins.

When I heard the instructor calling out that dolphins were now in the pen with us, I panicked a little, trying to remember all the "do's-and-don'ts" while intensely focusing on Rick, wondering how I had gotten myself into this situation. Suddenly, although I couldn't see a thing, I heard a lot of shouting.

Thinking something was wrong, I pulled off the goggles and saw the whole crew on the edge of the pen wildly waving their arms and pointing to a dolphin swimming in a circle around Rick and me. I stuck my head back under the water with my naked eye just in time to see the magnificent creature, inches away, gliding silently past us. In an unforgettable, slow-motion moment, we were eye-to-eye. Two artists linked by their commonality, each exploring a new and different world, encircled by a being of nature who sensed distress and came to help.

Eye of the Dolphin

If only we could each be the dolphin when encountering one another in our movements through this life, being to being, eye to eye. •

Arlene Mandell is an artist living in Linville, North Carolina. Her engaging portraits can be seen year-round at the Carlton Gallery in Banner Elk. Relocating two years ago from Miami to the Grandfather Mountain community inspired a love of writing. She is a member of the North Carolina Poetry Society and also Sue Spirit's Writing Workshop in Vilas. Her essays and poems have appeared in *Second Spring* and *Gateways* literary anthologies.

The Shot Heard Round My World
by James R. Mullis

*ing, ring.*

"Hello."

"James, I know you and the family are on a trip…But you need to come home now…"

If I had been there, could I have made a difference? How could I not see this coming? Nothing makes sense right now. Find the pieces, all the missing pieces of this puzzle. I know they are there. Look harder! Search for the signs. There had to be signs, but I have missed them somehow. Oh, how could I miss the signs? Wait, good grief, did I miss the signs, or did I just not want to see them?

Honk, honk.

Pay attention! Stay in your lane! You have to drive from the hills of Tennessee to the piedmont of North Carolina as quickly as possible! Check your speed, check your mirrors, check…on your family! Just glance around the van at your wife and kids. No direct eye contact or you will lose it. How am

I going to explain this to them, when I do not understand it myself?

Oh, my God, I am hurting, I am confused; no, I am pissed off! This is stupid! I should not have to deal with this, much less try to help my family deal with this. Listen to their sobs. Look at their tears. Keep it together, James. Be strong…for them. They need you to be their rock, now more than ever.

Oh no, my mom? She is at your brother's house. He will take care of her until you arrive. Just drive! Texas…my brother, my niece, my nephew? I have to call and tell them. How? How do you explain this? They are 1100 miles away. Who will be there for them? This is not fair!

Such an idiot! I cannot believe this! Why, why, why? So selfish, so incredibly selfish! No, do not scream. Not now. Not in front of your family. Turn on the radio. Maybe the artist can sing away the ambience of pain that is filling the van. Breathe…in slowly, then out slowly. Focus, man, focus. Check your speed, check your mirrors, almost at the halfway point. Keep driving.

So much to do. So many calls to make. Help! But who is going to help me? It falls to me now. It is my responsibility. I did not ask for this! I am so mad right now! How dare…coward! This has caused immense pain. Check on the family, offer them a few comforting words. Comforting words? What are those words? My mouth will not even shape those words right now. But your family needs those words. Come on, you can do this. They need to know that everything is going to be alright. Really? Is it going to be alright? When? James, stop this!

Enough self-pity! Focus man. Check your speed, check your mirrors, just a few more miles.

No, no, no, hold back the tears. There will be time to cry later. Where are the pieces that I missed? Come on James, think! If I had known that this were going to happen, I would never have taken this trip. I would have never gone so far away. Why this? Why now? Spineless imbecile! I feel such anger right now! This is too much! Breathe…slowly. Grandpa! Oh my God! How am I going to tell my grandpa that his only son has…?

"Mr. Mullis, I'm the chief detective. I am returning your dad's 357 revolver to you. Please sign here. And Mr. Mullis, I must warn you, it is still in the evidence bag. It has not been cleaned. It is just as we found it next to his body."

From the lonely bridge that arched his mind
To the darkest depths he hurled.
Where his soul in agony did grind
Silenced by the shot heard round my world.

Triumph from tragedy! Refusal to languish in the misery of my father's suicide prompted me to action. I did not want the pain of this tragedy to be in vain. In my spirit I longed to ensure positive results from such a heartbreaking loss. During those dark days a thought sparked, and a scripture surfaced: "Have compassion, make a difference." Thus, the Jude 22 Ministry was born with the purpose of assisting in the mental health outreach aspect of our community. This program is designed

The Shot Heard Round My World

to help individuals and families whose lives have been impacted by suicide. Our desire is to bind the wounds, comfort the hurting, show compassion, and make a difference. •

James R. Mullis lives in Rockwell, North Carolina. He is the founder of the Jude22 Charity. A perpetual student, lecturer, coffee connoisseur, and avid reader. He is a dynamic speaker with a flair for storytelling and theatrics. He now brings that passion to the printed page.

Thundering Hooves
in the Land of Giants

by Suzanne Cottrell

I squirmed in my car seat and tapped my feet on the floor-board hurriedly as my husband and I drove into the National Bison Range in Montana. We opened our eyes wider. Exhilaration or fear? Probably both. I had only seen bison in a zoo, and only a few at that, so I was eager to gaze on a herd estimated at over 300 of the giants. We soon spied a cloud of ocher dust rising in the distance against the rugged peaks of the Mission Mountain Range.

As we approached the crest of a hill, two young bulls along the road grunted their disapproval at our territorial intrusion. They lowered their heads and pawed at the ground. My pulse quick-ened; my muscles tensed. These formidable beasts were unpredictable. I felt quite vulnerable seated in a rented Chevy Monza. In a charge, their massive, horned heads could crush our car like an aluminum can or easily flip it over. My knuckles whitened as I gripped the edge of the car seat and prayed under my breath, "Please stay put. We are not a threat." We kept a close eye on the pair as my husband advanced the car slowly along Prairie Drive, a 14-mile loop following Mission

Creek, where bison both drank and muddied the waters. We drove away from the agitated young bulls. I raised my face heavenward and whispered, "Thank you."

The creek along our route was bordered by a natural fence of thick buckthorn and coyote brush. Without warning, my husband stomped the brakes abruptly. I slammed forward, caught by my seat belt. I gasped. Enormous humps of dirty, matted brown fur plowed through the coyote brush like powerful locomotives. They bolted across the road into the meadow, wet mud coating their lower legs. The ground trembled beneath their thundering hooves. Their deep bellows resounded, reverberating in our vehicle. My adrenaline surged; my stomach became queasy.

"That was a close call," my husband declared, holding fast to the steering wheel. He raised his eyebrows and his voice. "I don't think they saw us."

"Either that or they're not intimidated by cars," I offered. "Do you think it's safe to drive on?" My heart pounded. I wrung my hands.

"We don't have much choice. This section of the road is one-way. I'll drive slowly, stay alert." His voice was reassuring. He eased his foot off the brake. The speedometer inched up to 25 mph.

We scanned both sides of the road, listening intently for any warning signals—a snort or a grunt. What I thought was going to be an intriguing adventure among free-roaming bison in the

Montana countryside was a nerve-wracking game of hide-and-seek. Although close encounters with the bison excited me, the thought of a one-ton animal ramming into the side of the car terrified me.

Our Chevy crept up the ascending roadway. Reaching a plateau, we pulled into a scenic overlook. Still fearful of a stray monstrous creature charging at 35 mph, we chose not to get out of the car. Instead, we opened our car windows for a better look. We enjoyed the spiced-honey aroma of Blue Elderberries and the piney, citrusy scent of the Monterey Pines especially preferred over the musky odor of bison.

Now at a safe distance, I appreciated the opportunity to observe these magnificent creatures. At least 50 bison grazed on rye grass and wild oats in the valley below. The cows and their calves moved along, grazing methodically. I thought about a time when millions of bison populated the western prairies and waves of brown, shaggy beasts foraged on meadows of barley and wild rye. They must have been a compelling sight. I recalled reading how valuable bison were to Native Americans for meat and hides.

A pair of frisky calves shook their heads and galloped as if playing a game of tag. My husband and I chuckled at their antics. The cows tried to corral the youngsters, reminding me of teachers gathering their students at the end of recess. We noticed a few mule deer on the fringe of the bison herd; we could hear a bald eagle squawk overhead. I envisioned a startled herd stampeding, trampling everything in its path. I imagined the deafening sound of pounding hooves, clouds of choking dust, flying clumps of grass, and massive silhouettes casting long shadows across the plains.

As we pulled back onto the road to drive the last segment of the loop, I wondered what would keep this herd of 300 from being startled by a passing car of curious visitors. The massive size and power of the bison commanded my respect, but I was not relieved until our tiny car passed unscathed through the final gate of the National Bison Range beyond the world of these giants. •

Suzanne Cottrell, a member of the Granville Writers' Group and North Carolina Writers' Network, lives with her husband and three rescue dogs in Granville County, North Carolina. An outdoor enthusiast and retired teacher, she enjoys reading, writing, knitting, hiking, Pilates, and yoga. Her prose has appeared in numerous journals and anthologies, including *Bearing Up*, *Pop Machine*, *Unwanted Visitors*, *Empty Silos*, *Dragon Poet Review*, *Dual Coast Magazine*, *Parks and Points*, and *Nailpolish Stories*.

Into the Woods

by Marshall McClung

I have been an admirer of Daniel Boone since reading about him as a child. While I do not consider myself to be anywhere close to having the woodsman skills Boone had, I do believe I have certain traits Boone would be proud of.

I was born and reared in a log cabin at the edge of Cherokee Indian land in Graham County, North Carolina. My playground was the woods, my playmates Cherokee children playing "Cowboys and Indians" and reversing the roles. Nobody was offended. I later had a career with the U.S. Forest Service that honed my skills; my love for the woods ever deepened.

I first became involved in search-and-rescue operations while working with the U.S. Forest Service and later as Search-and-Rescue Coordinator with the Graham County Rescue Squad. We looked mostly for lost and injured hikers in the Joyce Kilmer-Slickrock Wilderness Area in Graham County. The number of those missions is now in the hundreds spread over more than 50 years.

I use tracking skills to find lost hikers partly learned on my own and also from attending tracking school and becoming a certified tracker. I have found or helped find hundreds of lost and injured hikers using these skills. The skills enable one to discover extremely minor details when tracking a person.

I look for footprints, broken twigs, small rocks that have been moved by a person's foot, discarded items, and other signs. Other indicators include where a person has slipped and fallen or left the trail. A smaller footprint can mean a young person or a female. If the tracks start getting closer together and if the person is slipping and sliding more, we know they are getting exhausted. Or maybe they are not paying attention to where they are going. If the tracks change direction frequently, the person is confused and doesn't know which way to go. A larger disturbed area or depression in the leaves is an indication the person has sat or lain down.

A person almost always bends a twig in the direction they are going. If the twig is bent on the right side of the trail, the person is right-handed; if on the left side, they are left-handed. If the person has entered a stream, we search both sides of the stream until we locate footprints on the bank where they left the stream. If they are in a rocky area, small bits of grit or pieces of stones leave scratch marks on the rocks. The scratch marks will be deeper closest to the person because as a person steps on this type of surface, the foot tends to slip slightly toward the walker. Trackers can use this to determine which way the person is going.

One mission that stands out in my memory was a search in the autumn of 1988. We were searching for Jim Michelic, 25, of

New Berlin, Wisconsin. That search lasted almost a month. Michelic entered the Joyce Kilmer-Slickrock Area and disappeared. When he failed to return as planned, a massive search effort began. "Hoot" Gibbs and I found his tent on Stratton Bald, but no sign that anyone had been there recently. Heavy rains had wiped out footprints. After days of searching by ground crews, search dogs, and aircraft, the search was suspended.

On October 16, two local fishermen taking a shortcut through dense underbrush found a backpack and boots at the base of a cliff. This was literally in the middle of nowhere. The items were identified by relatives as belonging to Michelic. The following day, the fishermen led us to the location where they had found the items. After a short search, we located the scattered remains of Michelic. It was later determined that a bear had eaten most of the remains. An autopsy revealed that Michelic had died as a result from injuries received from the fall.

During my years of wandering and searching through the forests of Graham County, I've had my share of interesting finds, quite often made with my hiking friend "Hoot" Gibbs.

We found all of the original route of the Trail of Tears in Graham County used for removing Cherokee Indians in 1838 and the burial mounds of 400-some Cherokees who died in a 1700's small pox epidemic. We found several graves of children who died from Milk Sick Fever before 1916 in Eller Cove and Spanish writing carved into a rock at Hooper Bald: "Predarms Casada, Sep. 1615."

The forest and wilderness can be a foreboding place to some, but the truth is humankind has been wandering about the world for centuries. If you know what to look for—and if you don't get lost—you might find evidence of any number of interesting stories nearby when you next venture into the woods. •

Marshall McClung is a prominent local historian in Graham County, North Carolina. He has written many stories published in the Graham Star, Robbinsville's newspaper. Marshall has published two books: *Mountain People - Mountain Places* which received an award from the North Carolina Society of Historians, Inc. In 2018, he released *More Mountain People - Mountain Places*. Marshall has assisted many other writers in publishing books, most recently Marci Spencer who released *Nantahala National Forest, A History* in 2017.

Alvin and Mrs. Moody

by Joel Stegall

T he first day of sixth grade was perhaps the single most
memorable day of my elementary school life.

I dreaded going back to school that fall. The spring before, my
daddy, the pastor of the Baptist church right across the road
from the school, had been asked to resign. Everyone knew we
were going to move. We just didn't know where or when.
Daddy had first to locate a church that wanted him. Unlike the
Methodists who re-assigned clergy when their welcome had
worn out, a Baptist pastor who had been asked to leave was on
his own to find a new church. As the end of the summer
approached and nothing had turned up for Daddy, I was more
than a little apprehensive about having to explain to school
friends why we had not moved.

On the day fall classes began, I walked across the road to the
schoolyard well before the opening bell. I met kids I had not
seen all summer. None of them asked why I was still there.
However, in the hallway on the way to homeroom, one of the
teachers—a church member who had helped engineer Daddy's
resignation—saw me and blurted out, "What are you doing

here?" Maybe she was innocently asking for information, but I was mortified. I got over it soon enough because the matter did not come up again.

Alvin, who sat beside me in homeroom, was not so lucky. He had just moved to the community and no one knew him. Our homeroom teacher, Mrs. Moody, also new to the school, made it clear right up front that she was not to be trifled with. She obviously knew that sixth graders, especially boys, could be loud, obnoxious, and troublesome; in other words, such lads were given to age-appropriate behavior. One of the first opportunities for mischief came when Mrs. Moody told us to put both hands on our desktops so she could check them. I don't know what she was looking for. Maybe some contagious skin disease was going around. Like a stern drill instructor, she moved from desk to desk inspecting our hands, turning them over to see both sides, occasionally murmuring approval or concern.

When she got to Alvin, he obediently put his right hand on the desk but keep his left hand suspiciously in his lap. Mrs. Moody decided she had to take control before things got out of hand. Maybe Alvin was hiding something, she thought. A frog or a snake? Or maybe one of those books whose full-color, graphic portrayals of violent fantasy threatened the moral fiber of my generation—you know, comic books such as Batman, Superman, and The Lone Ranger?

Mrs. Moody just had to assert her authority. She said, in the hard, demanding voice that used to be required of all certified teachers, "Alvin, I said put both hands on the desk." But Alvin, like the Tar Baby in the Uncle Remus story, just sat there and didn't say anything. Whatever Alvin was up to, Mrs. Moody was having none of it. In an even sterner voice, she commanded, "Alvin, I said put both hands on your desk." But Alvin just silently stared straight ahead and did not move a muscle.

Mrs. Moody was running out of options and patience. In that place and time, paddling by the principal in front of the class was considered an appropriate last resort for teachers trying to get rebellious boys in line. In exasperation, Mrs. Moody declared, "Alvin, you're asking for a paddling." She reached under the desk to grab whatever Alvin was hiding in his hand. Mrs. Moody recoiled suddenly, flinching in horror as she felt the limp dead weight of a withered, immobile arm, one deformed since birth.

In that brief, terrible moment, truth broke through the boundaries of age and power. A few seconds earlier, the relationships had been polarized, confrontational. She was the teacher, we were the students. She gave orders, we obeyed or rebelled. But when truth exploded in our little classroom world, hostile confrontation was transformed into a mixture of confusion, bewilderment, and embarrassment. Compassion may have sneaked in also.

If I could be a playwright and revise the script for that day's drama, would I? In a heartbeat, yes. But I also learned some important things.

What you think is an objective inquiry can be experienced by someone else as a personal intrusion. And, having greater authority doesn't mean you have all the facts. Moreover, someone's lack of response does not always indicate insolence. Sometimes things turn out better than we expect, and sometimes worse. And that's why our most difficult days can be those when we learn the most. •

As a music professor and academic administrator, Joel Stegall authored more than 35 journal articles, book chapters, and other such long-forgotten documents. Since retiring to Winston-Salem, North Carolina, he has completed a family history dating from the early Colonial Era. Delighted to discover in his bloodline ingenuity, inventiveness, devotion to duty, self-sacrifice and uncommon love, he was at the same time distressed to find insanity, murder, suicide, and cattle rustling.

Grandma's Shoebox

by Marie Mitchell

I t's a tradition at Eastern Kentucky University for students who are worried about a test, performance, or upcoming game, to stop by the 7-foot bronze statue of Daniel Boone in front of the Keen Johnson Building and to rub his toe for good luck. The toe has a nice brassy shine to it thanks to these heartfelt—sometimes desperate—pleas for help. Even Fess Parker, who portrayed Boone on TV, gave the toe a pat when he was visiting the Richmond campus in 1968.

Does it work? Hard to say. But it reassures those superstitious folks who have nothing to lose.

I could have used some form of divine intervention my first semester of college, back in the '70s. I was lost. Intimidated. Overwhelmed.

It was remarkable that I even enrolled since I'd almost dropped out of high school my senior year. I'd recently transferred from a school with 60 students in my class to one with 2,000. I didn't fit in. Was bored with classes. And school seemed a waste of time. My teachers and guidance counselor had low expectations of me, but I toughed it out and graduated. That's something my sisters and I were the first in our family to do.

Now what? I didn't want to stay home and work in a junk-mail factory. Or any other factory. Job options were extremely limited in my small Iowa town. So, given those dim prospects, I applied to college. And was shocked to be accepted.

My parents, neither with high school diplomas, helped me pack my things. Drove me from southeast Iowa to northeast Missouri. Unloaded the car. Fed me. Wished me good luck. And headed home.

Leaving me alone. In a new place. Far from family. Where I didn't know a soul. Didn't have a clue. And was consumed by second thoughts that I didn't really belong there.

The tiny dorm room, stacked with boxes of clothes, school supplies and other necessities, seemed empty. Cold. Uninviting.

My roommate, whom I'd corresponded with, wasn't coming until the next day. So there was no one to talk to. This was when a long-distance phone call was reserved for emergencies and long before cell phones. Or FaceTime. So, in a dorm full of girls, I felt lonely. Isolated. Scared.

To calm myself, I began to unpack shirts, shoes, toiletries, binders, and pens. Tucked away in the larger boxes was a smaller shoebox my Grandma Ruby had handed me before I left. I was too absorbed with saying good-bye to give it much thought then.

Now, curious, I carefully opened the Earth Shoe shoebox. Inside I found seven individually-wrapped packages with a different day of the week written on each.

I selected Sunday. Held it. Studied it. Decided to peek inside. Found stationery. With stamps. A subtle reminder to write home. And making it easy to follow through.

That small gift spoke volumes. Somebody cared about this frightened girl on her own at college, hundreds of miles from home. Grandma, with an eighth-grade education, believed I could do the work, earn the degree, and pursue a career. This blind faith boosted my spirits. Got me through the night. Gave me the courage to continue.

The first week of school that followed was challenging. Finding classrooms. Buying textbooks. Writing assignments. Choosing friends. Coping on my own.

But every day when I returned to my dorm room, I looked forward to opening the next gift. There was Avon perfume. A picture of Grandma and me by her strawberry patch. A column clipped from Dear Abby about postponing sex until marriage. And on day seven, a $10 bill to celebrate.

My excitement about the gifts wasn't because of what was in the packages. They just served as a reassuring reminder that someone thought I was special.

Grandma's gentle gesture of support made a lasting impression on me. I managed to earn both a Bachelor's and Master's

Grandma's Shoebox

71

degree after barely completing high school. And, when my nieces and nephew went off to college, I packed each one a shoebox. Filled with goofy things. Silly pictures. Tantalizing treats. Some stuffed animal dressed in their school colors. Always money on the seventh day.

When my own kids started college, I did the same for them. Even for the son who attended the local college and lived at home his freshman year.

The exact gifts they won't remember. But with a little luck, they'll never forget that the presents were wrapped in faith with love. It might be enough to tackle life's challenges knowing someone believed they were smart, brave and adventurous enough to succeed. •

Marie Mitchell is a former journalist who retired after 24 years as News Director of WEKU-FM, Eastern Kentucky University's public radio station in Richmond. She now teaches public speaking at EKU. Marie has co-authored four Kentucky-based books for young readers with her husband, Mason Smith, and two with Rebecca Mitchell Turney. Collaborating with four other EKU professors, Marie has co-written nine adult novels under the pen name Quinn MacHollister. All books are available on Amazon.

We Who Are Nobody

by Bohdan Dziadyk

A t the close of World War II, Europe was in a state of upheaval and ferment. Millions of "Ostarbeiters," that is, "eastern workers," who had been forced by the Germans from their homelands into slave labor for the Third Reich, were newly liberated. They had a sense of vast relief but also deep concerns of uncertainty about the future. Among these millions, Ivan Dziadyk met Maria Jaroszuk. They had labored for years in the ball bearing plants of Schweinfurt, in northwest Bavaria, and had survived its being bombed repeatedly by the U.S. Eighth Air Force in England. They married and had three children. After the U.S. Congress passed the Displaced Persons Acts of 1948 and 1950, that family was able to immigrate to the United States. My parents, my siblings, and I arrived through Ellis Island in October 1950. That same night we were on a train bound for Alton, Illinois.

Our first house in America was a rented, two-bedroom structure that depended on a wood stove for heating and cooking. The bathroom was an outdoor privy. I recall the rent was about $30 per month in the early 1950s. Dad worked at first in a butcher shop and then got a job in a steel mill where he would remain for 30 years, retiring at age 62. It was dirty, difficult, and sometimes dangerous work, but with his limited education and a family to care for, it was the best he could do.

America, in turns, amazed, amused, and sometimes appalled my parents, but they were always impressed at its sheer productivity and opportunity for those who were prepared. Neither of my parents had more than three years of formal education in their Ukrainian homeland. Dad would lament late in life that a lack of education had held him back, although he achieved as much or more than some of our neighbors who were high school graduates. I came to understand that some-times character could make as much difference in life as education or raw talent. My parents had individually been tested severely in their youth and had learned how to endure and to survive.

In 1954, the year I started first grade, our family purchased a small home closer to the Laclede Steel plant where Dad worked. For years he labored to renovate and enlarge our house. I remember the pipes often freezing in winter and the effort required to thaw them out. We maintained a garden in the back yard which provided vegetables and thus reduced our food expenses. We children - a second daughter was born in 1960 - grew up there, and both Mom and Dad died there some 40 years later.

Near the end of his life and after Mom had died, Dad and I were sharing a glass of bourbon one hot afternoon and reminiscing. He offered a simple but eloquent summary of his life, "I am always quiet, humble, but a good worker and a good

Christian." When comparing himself to native-born Americans he would say, "We have to always remember we are foreigners." The implication was they were low on the social ladder and could expect little better in their social standings. Along with the destitute millions of others displaced from their European homelands, Dad and Mom were "nobodies" but only to those who could not understand or value "the salt of the earth."

In any idyllic sense, they were far from perfect. I remember screaming spats and name-calling from the daily stresses, the agony of their war memories and the separation from relatives, for once we left Europe, they never saw a relative again and neither did we children. We grew up without so much as ever saying "Hi" to a cousin or "I love you" to a grandparent. Mom especially suffered for decades from loneliness for her homeland and from isolation from normal human contact. From time to time, she spent a week or so in a mental hospital battling her demons. Her prayer book brought from Europe was her constant companion, providing the little solace she could find in life. In the eyes of middle-class America, Ivan and Maria Dziadyk may have seemed little more than backward illiterates. To me, considering what they had endured in their native Ukraine, survived in Nazi Germany, and modestly but solidly achieved in America, they were the finest people I have ever known. I do not consider myself their equal. •

After serving in the U.S. Army for three years as a Special Forces medic, Bohdan Dziadyk completed M.S. and Ph.D. degrees in botany and ecology. For 36 years, he was a professor of biology at Augustana College in Rock Island, Illinois. Since retiring in 2016, he has maintained his interests in environmental studies and natural history.

Two Good Swings

by Landis Wade

In the fictional movie, *Little Big Man*, Dustin Hoffman played 121-year-old Jack Crabb, a white man with a remarkable but hard-to-believe life story set against the backdrop of the Great American West. Jack was only 10-years-old in 1859 when his family was murdered and the Cheyenne captured him. A few years later, the white-boy-turned-Indian was captured again, this time by the U.S. Army. Jack didn't know where he belonged or who he wanted to be as he comically and tragically stumbled from one occupation to the next. He first tried apprenticing to a snake-oil salesman, until the tar and feathers led him to become a gunslinger who couldn't shoot straight. General store owner, town drunk, muleskinner and cavalry scout for General George Armstrong Custer rounded out Jack's idiosyncratic career, where, in the end, Jack became the only white survivor at The Little Big Horn before he returned to the Cheyenne.

My life has not been so cinematic, but like Jack Crabb in search of his calling, I had a decision to make in 1979 and I didn't have a clue as to how to make it. After graduating from a respected liberal arts college with a degree in history, all I had to do was "decide" what to do with my life. I suffered as the only young person in the free world flustered by the question, the only boy who couldn't figure out how to become a man. I was jealous of friends who had planned ahead and knew exactly what they wanted to "be." Me? I hadn't planned ahead. I made decent grades, walked across the graduation stage, and looked up to stare into the unknown, trying to understand a world where they no longer handed out a syllabus and gave you graded feedback. I experienced a culture shift called adulthood. And for the next twelve months of my life—which I kiddingly told my friends was my long-planned "year-off"— I did one thing after the other, tasting jobs like they were different flavors of candy, never settling on one that tasted any good. I became "Little Big Man."

Sure, I was not captured, recaptured, or tarred and feathered, but it felt like it. I had to find a job. One with a purpose. In the meantime? Any job would do.

My first job was a two-month internship at a government think tank, but after I completed my first assignment in one week, I got a disapproving lecture from a career bureaucrat. My work was fine. What was wrong was that the project was supposed to last all summer. Disillusioned, I watched grass grow on the taxpayer-funded lawn outside my window for the next seven weeks, at which point I had to get outside. I took a construction job working for $2.25 an hour with a crew that didn't think much of education. My on-site boss without a high school degree called me "college boy" every time he had me fetch something.

In *Little Big Man*, Jack Crabb walked blindly from one job to the next, which was how I fell into a series of jobs that didn't require a college degree. Much like a snake-oil salesman, I tried to unload coupon books on unsophisticated consumers. With the panache of a general-store owner and cavalry scout, I waited tables for hungry customers and delivered furniture to hard-to-find places. When I became depressed, I didn't buy a gun like Jack-the-gunslinger, but I did buy enough six-packs to make Jack-the-town-drunk proud. I plodded from job to job like a mule being poked by a muleskinner, until I ended up, once again, doing manual labor on a construction site. And that is when it happened, at about 6:45 a.m. one morning.

The ground was frozen solid, and the temperature was in the single digits. My task was to drive a steel stake into the ground with a sledgehammer. After several whacks, I was getting nowhere, so I took a big arching swing with one arm, holding the stake with the other hand. It was the swing that changed my life for more than three decades. I missed the stake and hit my thumb. And right then and there, on a cold and frosty morning, I made up my mind. I would become a lawyer. Not to change the world. Not to make a difference. But because it was better than the alternative.

––––––––––––––––––––––––––

This decision to become a lawyer was the right call. It allowed me to grow up and do some good, but after 35 years, it's time for me to take another swing. And this time, if all goes well, it will lead to a tale about a lawyer-turned-storyteller who lived to be 121 years old. •

Landis Wade is a recovering trial lawyer, author, and producer/host of Charlotte Readers Podcast (www.charlottereaderspodcast.com). His third book, *The Christmas Redemption*, won the Holiday category in the 12th Annual National Indie Excellence Awards. He won the 2016 North Carolina State Bar short story contest for "The Deliberation" and received awards in 2017 and 2018 for non-fiction pieces, "The Cape Fear Debacle" and "First Dance." "Shelby" appeared in the 2018 Personal Essay Publishing Project anthology *Bearing Up*.

Return to Gap Creek

by Marion Hodge

I like maps—I've read them and drawn them since I was a kid—but sometimes I prefer just walking into the unknown; I learn something—especially about myself. At the end of *Walden*, in which he examines his own values and beliefs, Henry David Thoreau asks us to do the same, to seek and map the "streams" of our own inner worlds, to be the "Lewis and Clark" of ourselves, to explore our "own higher latitudes," our highest ideals.

Exploring one's interior world, Thoreau believes, is more important than exploring the exterior one, for too often and too long our inner worlds remain "white," unexplored, on the "chart," the map, of our souls. We know too little about our own identities. Still, as his metaphor indicates, discoveries we make in the exterior world can serve us well as symbols and models for making spiritual discoveries. Such has been one continuing experience in my life, one that connects me to my own higher ground.

I grew up along Gap Creek at Elizabethton, Tennessee, in a house now moved to make room for a new four-lane Gap

Creek Road/Mary Patton Highway extension. Our house was about a half-mile as the crow flies from the mouth of the creek in the Watauga River, about four-hundred yards from the original site of Fort Watauga where settlers survived an attack and siege in 1776, about a mile from Sycamore Shoals where patriots mustered as militia to fight the British at King's Mountain in 1780. As a youth, I often saw in my imagination that long column of citizen-soldiers riding on the other side of the creek, heading south. I got an idea of the creek's importance at even earlier times when I found arrowheads along its banks.

At first the creek was a child's "backyard" playground. We waded in it. Where a huge tree urged it to change course and scrape the bed away into a kind of "hole," we could swim a few strokes in it. We made battlegrounds for our plastic "army men," with machinegun "pill-boxes" of sticks and the sand it brought downstream—and when we had firecrackers we made "explosions." We built dams across it. We discovered and "played with" minnows, spotted salamanders, and what we called crawfish and water spiders (which seemed to walk on water). We caught black snakes with our bare hands. Sluggish they were when molting. We feared stumbling upon water moccasins and copperheads. We were disgusted by foot-long beady-eyed water rats. On its banks and in the darkness of maples, hickories, oaks, sycamores, elms, tulip poplars, we played hide-and-seek, cowboys and Indians, Davy Crockett, army.

Later the creek became the source of wonder and mystery—about what lay beyond sight upstream—about creation and divinity. Birds in their myriad colors and songs became oracles of beauty and harmony. Reading Walt Whitman brought ideas of unity, coherence. I would walk up the creek in snow, and feel—what?—something close and holy in the ice on dormant stalks of plants. All the creek provided had become miracle.

And now, in old age, I have renewed those bonds with Gap Creek. I have done so after two years on active duty as a soldier, and after a long career teaching college composition, literature, and creative writing courses, grading papers and exams—the most deadening grades those that must be assigned a poem, an expression of a student's very spirit, but I just could not put "A" on all of them—serving on faculty committees, evaluating courses, programs, junior professors, writing scholarly essays and poems, and trying to get them published, making presentations at professional conferences.

The Gap Creek land we lived on, I've discovered, was originally owned by one of the earliest settlers, Matthew Talbot, who had a grist mill up the creek a mile or so from our gone house, along a segment of an old wagon road. I've found several worked stones along the creek where the mill stood, limestone cut and drilled by the hands of earlier residents and workers. The stones remind me of the arrowheads worked by even earlier residents. They remind me of the work my brother Bill, a master carpenter, has done, and the work my brother Randy, an accomplished artist, has done. We are not very different, after all, from each other, whether we abided there two thousand years ago, or two-hundred, or twenty.

Sometimes to flee the mundane, I return to the creek, though two hundred miles away, again squat alongside, watch it and listen to it, reflect amid its reflections of the deep sky. As a boy, I didn't know where it came from. Now I have explored its springs and tributaries—upstream, up there on Stone Mountain, higher ground. •

Marion Hodge lives in High Point, North Carolina. He holds degrees from East Tennessee State University, where he was an ROTC Distinguished Military Student, and the University of Tennessee, Knoxville. He has published numerous poems and scholarly essays. While teaching at High Point University for 30 years, he was granted the Ridenhour Scholarly and Professional Achievement Award; the university has also named a student creative writing award in his honor.

Searching for Paradise
by Alice Osborn

The Donner Party. Snow. Starvation. Cannibalism. Why does this tragedy from 172 years ago obsess me today? I'm fascinated with any story about extreme weather, foolish choices, poor leadership, unexpected heroes, and people who dream about making a better life, but die on the road to achieving it. I don't have an ancestor from the Donner Party, but my father's family, who came to America in the 17th and 18th centuries from England and the Netherlands, wanted everything the Donners did: new hope for their families while securing a strong financial future for their children. We want the same things in America today.

Like their great-grandparents and my ancestors who fled the Old Country, the Donner brothers packed up their lives to discover a more prosperous tomorrow in California. George and his brother Jacob, born in Rowan County, North Carolina, had already moved to build better farms in Kentucky, Indiana, and Illinois, and now California had the promise of more land, easier weather, and a career opportunity for George's wife, Tamsen. She was George's junior by twenty years and had suffered greatly when she was a school teacher in Elizabeth

City, North Carolina, where her two young children and husband all died from disease. Fate and timing led her to Sangamon County, Illinois, where she married twice-widowed George, and became a step-mother to Leanna and Elitha, and mother to Georgia, Frances, and Eliza. She loved being a mother, but wanted to return to teaching, so she made plans to start a girls' seminary in California. Along the 2,000-mile journey, Tamsen carefully drew and recorded all of the wild-flowers and other flora she met along the wagon trail in her journal. Sadly, her journal and her body were never recovered from the camp where she spent her last winter with her family.

Last summer, I fell headlong into Tamsen Donner, who hit all of the marks as I created a new folk song: North Carolina ties, a tragic end, a bold story of sacrifice. I felt I could have been friends with her. Tamsen knew it was a bad idea to follow the Hastings Cut-off through the Wasatch Mountains and Great Salt Lake Desert of Utah instead of following the well-traveled Oregon Trail. She felt Lansford Hastings' much-touted short cut written about in the *Emigrants' Guide to Oregon and California* was nothing more than a scam to get emigrants to buy over-priced goods at Fort Bridger. Unfortunately, no one listened to her and the short cut cost the Donner Party many valuable days and cattle, setting them up to be stranded in the Sierra Nevadas because the high snows wouldn't let them pass into California.

At Alder Creek, the Donner families and their teamsters fared much worse than their fellow emigrants who hunkered in cabins next to Truckee Lake six miles away. George had injured his hand while repairing a broken axle and that wound quickly became infected. Isolated with their oxen meat buried in 25-foot snow drifts, the dead accumulated, and Tamsen made the children eat their flesh to survive.

Tamsen kept her girls going by brushing their hair every day, reading to them, and assigning chores to keep life as close to normal in their snowy prison. The first rescue party arrived in February three and a half months after their path was blocked, but Tamsen refused to leave George, so she and her birth daughters stayed at camp. Finally, a month later Tamsen told the last rescue team, "Please save my children." She was never seen alive again, but all three girls made it safely through the mountains.

I wanted to write an honest song that addressed the choice of staying with a beloved partner versus leaving your young children potentially orphaned. As a mother of two, I know I couldn't leave my children, but this was Tamsen's song. And so, I wrote the chorus:

> *Paradise, guide us around the bend*
> *Please, let this winter end*
> *Stop the sky from falling*
> *The hurt from calling*
> *No, sir, I cannot leave*
> *Please save my children*
> *Some dreams weren't meant to be*

The rest of the song traces Tamsen's journey from hope to horror and then back to hope:

> *I hear hummingbirds, meadows warm in the sun*
> *Almost like Carolina where we come from*

Searching for Paradise

I float over the cabins and creek
Girls—you've made it to Paradise without me

Tamsen's dream died, yet all of her girls lived long, reasonably healthy lives, and gave her grandchildren because she inspired them to see the beauty amongst the decay, and the hope amongst the fear. She gave them strength to carry on and it's through this strength that I make meaning from her life and her sacrifice every time I sing her song. •

Alice Osborn from Raleigh, North Carolina, is a multi-genre author, singer-songwriter, and editor-for-hire whose most recent CD is *Old Derelicts*; her poetry collections include *Heroes without Capes*, *After the Steaming Stops*, and *Unfinished Projects*. Alice loves writing songs about American history that frequently return to the themes of home, identity, and yearning. Her family has deep roots going back before the Revolution. She also plays Celtic fiddle and bluegrass banjo. Visit Alice's website at www.aliceosborn.com.

The Plummet

by Susan Wilson

Aging never scared me. But my opponent has proven far more powerful, more devious, and less fair-minded than I anticipated. I expected aging to arrive as a gradual decline and to be able to navigate the gentle downward slope through planning and adherence to healthy personal habits. Instead, the experience has been an unrelenting downhill slide that has felt more like jumping off a cliff and bouncing off jagged rocks before plummeting into a shark infested pool where the only way out is the obvious one. Slowly being eaten alive, one bite at a time.

At first, I barely noticed. My attacker was subtle. Little lines that were not altogether unattractive appeared in gently increasing quantity. Should have used moisturizer earlier. Should have embraced paleness before it became stylish. Then came migration. Ounces of flesh and muscle and fat that once lived in a penthouse address suddenly looked for lower level accommodations. Spots, both light and dark, appeared, nothing approaching consistency, along with wrinkles that can never be smoothed and progressively grow deeper. None of this was unexpected, though perhaps more distressing than I had anticipated.

Then one by one, joints became uncooperative. Muscles, tendons, and cartilage piled on. I was stunned by the rapidity, then resolved to the inevitability. The neck went first. One vertebra crashing into the one below. My neurosurgeon advised against water skiing and roller coaster rides. Small price, minimal loss. The neck was swiftly followed by a shoulder, which I blamed on the neck, a pillow, and four different mattresses. Bless the Costco return policy. Then it was my low back. Ditto mattress. Ditto Costco. I lost weight, took up yoga, and quit bending over to garden and weed. The yard has not forgiven me quite yet. Eventually one knee began to protest followed somewhat reluctantly by the second. Both of them opposed to running, sitting, sleeping, and sudden movements to the left or right. I feel more than fortunate that knees, hips, and feet are still willing to put their personal needs aside and to work together to accommodate a morning walk. I'd like to think the worst is over, but it is likely only beginning.

I have not slept through the night in almost six years. Despite my multiple attempts, I have yet to purchase the magical mattress that can make worrisome thoughts and pressure points disappear. I do however have fingers, feet, and often complete limbs that quietly go to sleep without notice then protest painfully when awakened.

I am not overweight; I do not suffer from diabetes, or high blood pressure, nor am I battling a cancerous growth of which I am aware. I treat anxiety and depression with the thankfully-still-possible long walks and good books. If only I could age as slowly as Kinsey Millhone. The children are grown but have yet to deposit tiny, age-reversing bundles to occupy my free time, a prospect I once feared but now realize is simply nature's coping mechanism. Which still leaves me with opportunity to stop by a mirror and wonder if new lighting might help and sit quietly and internally debate the cost benefit of anti-aging creams.

I have always known I would grow old. I am surprised so many others lack this knowledge. Or do they just refuse to admit the opponent exists, believing the ability to ignore a suitable weapon? I do not live in denial injecting each line, nipping each bulge, tacking up each loose flap. I do not pretend that by shopping the right stores I can stay in the range of a perpetual twenty-one. I am not ashamed to embrace the ever-flattering black yoga pant as daily attire. I am growing fond of strategically placed ruching and garments that fit what remains and gently flow over what has been lost. Comfortable has become a word I seek out over form-fitting and figure-enhancing (code words for restrictive and tight).

My husband's answer to aging was to simply profess he did not plan to live past the age of sixty. It was also his retirement plan. And though he gave it admirable effort, cataract surgeries and social security checks await him. I thought I was organized and prepared for the challenge and yet clearly underestimated my adversary. Expecting a marathon swim, I never knew I'd need to learn how to dive. •

Susan Wilson lives in Clemmons, North Carolina, and is a member

The Plummet

of Winston-Salem Writers. Her creative nonfiction work has appeared in *Flying South* and *Bearing Up*. She was a finalist for the 2017 James Hurst Prize for fiction and a finalist for the 2018 North Carolina State University Shorter Fiction Prize. She is currently working on a collection of creative nonfiction.

He Fell Off His Mule and Died
by Joel Stegall

Although this story is about just one such man, the larger story it represents is about all the daring souls who braved the early American frontier to make a better life for themselves and their families.

The itinerant Baptist preacher/farmer set off on his mule one cold Sunday night for a service at one of his churches. Having travelled this Anson County, North Carolina, road too many times to count, neither man nor animal hesitated to ride alone through the woods in the dead of winter. Perhaps to fortify himself against the cold, perhaps to calm his erratic heart, or maybe simply because he liked the taste, Preacher Moses sipped a bit of the home brew he produced on his farm.

For people like me who grew up Southern Baptist in the mid-20th Century, it seems unthinkable that a Baptist preacher would drink liquor. But this was 1840, and things were different. Baptists did not condemn alcohol until the 1890s. In fact, it was not unusual for pre-Civil War Southern farmers, or even preachers, to maintain a private still.

As dusk settled around him, the 105-year-old man, aware that the evening of his own life was upon him, could well have drifted into reflection on his remarkable personal journey.

Moses was born in 1735 into the family of a Kent County, Virginia, farmer who was most likely illiterate. In the same year, in the same community, Augustine and Mary Ball Washington's little boy, George, turned three. A bit to the north in Pennsylvania, Squire and Sarah Boone watched their son, Daniel, take his first steps.

Born with a misshapen foot commonly called a "clubbed" foot, Moses was limited in some physical activities, but he worked hard and had an agile mind. He also spoke well and found that people paid attention. As a teenager, he began to think about becoming a preacher. He also wanted to own land and be better off financially than his papa had been. He surely noticed that some folks, such as the Washingtons, owned a lot of land and lived better. Determined to take advantage of the economic opportunities to the south and west, Moses set off for North Carolina, as soon as he was old enough.

It is not known exactly what Moses did in those early adult years, but he must have established himself as dependable and hard-working. Not only did he farm, he also became known as the "club-footed Baptist preacher."

As Colonial frustration with British rule turned into Revolution, Moses, like many colonists, appears not to have been sure it was a smart idea for backwoods farmers to take up arms against the most powerful military in the world. In May

1777, the newly-formed North Carolina Assembly passed an "Act for the Security of the State," which required all males to sign an oath of allegiance. Moses refused, but when a Chatham County court ordered him to pay a fine and leave the state, he had a change of heart and joined the Revolution.

After the war was over, Moses moved a hundred miles west to Anson County, taking advantage of land grants available to settlers in North Carolina's western frontier. Typically, parcels of 100 acres were awarded to individuals, plus another 100 acres for each additional family member. With at least ten children, Moses may have been granted more than a thousand acres. By 1787, around the time Alexander Hamilton, James Madison, and John Jay published *The Federalist Papers*, Moses owned substantial farm land near the current town of Wingate. While he farmed, he continued to preach.

As Moses rode to church that Sunday evening in 1840—according to family records—he fell off his mule and died. Did he lose his balance, perhaps a bit tipsy from the hooch, and die of injuries sustained in a fall? Did he have a heart attack or stroke? One tradition says he froze to death. While that seems unlikely in the relatively mild climate, it is possible. Whatever the cause of death, the preacher/farmer was prepared. His will provided for the distribution of several hundred acres of land and other possessions.

Moses the preacher/farmer had lived long and prospered, fulfilling what would become known as the "American Dream." He provided well for his family and left substantial property to his children. And he passed on to his later descendants something even more important: a good example of a life well-lived, guided by imagination, energy, and a willingness to take risks.

I am proud to be one of those descendants. Moses Stegall was my third great-grandfather. •

As a music professor and academic administrator, Joel Stegall authored more than 35 journal articles, book chapters, and other such long-forgotten documents. Since retiring to Winston-Salem, North Carolina, he has completed a family history dating from the early Colonial Era. Delighted to discover in his bloodline ingenuity, inventiveness, devotion to duty, self-sacrifice and uncommon love, he was at the same time distressed to find insanity, murder, suicide, and cattle rustling.

Fathers and Mothers
by Annette Collins

Each June I revisit memories of my father, born in 1898 in Ware, Massachusetts. His name was Alphonse Joseph Martin, Jr. His parents migrated from Canada and were non-English-speaking people, so Father was bi-lingual.

Even today I recall the smell of his cigars, Dutch Masters and White Owls. He was a quiet man, the only one in his large family who attended college. Father was a tool and die maker and worked for an electrical engineering company.

Dad served several tours of duty in the Army Air Corps as a radioman. He also served in the U.S. Naval Reserve. While stationed at Long Beach, California, he received commendations for being the first person to get through to the outside world with news of the earthquake as it was happening. "Disregarding his personal safety," his commendation said, he stayed at his station while the building was still shaking and then manned his post continuously for a week in March 1933 passing along critical information out of Long Beach

Father built a home-made radio station in the basement of our home. When I was a little girl, I would go into the basement and watch him using the Morse Code and talking to people all over the world. My father's handle was W1IFQ, and he taught me my name in Morse Code. I still remember it.

Father was 11 years older than Mother. As an only-child, I had everything: lessons—dance, baton, voice, piano—and nice clothes, a nice bedroom, a big yard, a dog, roller skates, a bicycle, a baby-sitter. But do not be envious; my mother always worked. And things are not always what they seem from the outside looking in.

Mother was an alcoholic. I believe this was inherited from her own father. That grandfather worked on the railroad and I am told he would come home and beat up my grandmother. My mother, along with her sisters, would hide their mother from him when he came home drunk. He was mean when he drank. Mother was sent out to work after the 5th grade of school as were all her sisters. Her first job was as a little maid, working for the owners of the local thread mill. When she turned 12, she worked for the thread mill. My mother's name was Emelia Beaudry, but she preferred to be called Emelie. She would bring her paychecks home and give them to her mother. In exchange, she would get 25-cents spending money for the week from her mother.

My mother's father, Felix Beaudry, was from a prominent Boston family. He died long before I was born. My grand-mother ran a boarding house in their large home. The story I was told was that one of the guests who lived there, an old woman, advised my grandmother to give Felix something that could cause a heart attack. Well, my grandfather did die of a heart attack. There were no autopsies back then. I will go to my grave never knowing the truth of that story.

My own father, Alphonse, was my hero. When my mother drank, she became mean. As I recall, it was every other weekend at first. She only drank in the house, never in a bar. No one knew she drank but my father and me. She was mean to him when she drank. He would retreat to the basement, to his quiet place, his ham radio. I went with him or hid under my bed or in the closet.

Father loved to hunt, to fish, to play baseball. We used to go to the woods and gather nuts and bring a picnic lunch when he went fishing. Some weekends we went to the ocean, clamming, while father fished. Those were the happy times.

Father attended all my recitals, whether it was a voice recital at the Sessions Mansion in Bristol, Connecticut, or a dance recital at one of the local high schools. Mother was quiet and beautiful. I feared her when she drank.

My father died at age 65. Mother was 54. When Mother turned 70, she was cursed with cognitive issues so she could no longer live alone. This was a curse and a blessing. The curse was that she spent 18 years with this disease. The blessing was that God took away her desire for alcohol. In the years following her illness, I got to know and love her more than ever.

Every life has a story, every life meaning. We live our own

forward with heart and courage intertwined perhaps with parents and those who came before them. We understand those lives only when looking back with love and compassion—for those others and for ourselves. •

Annette Collins lives in Winston Salem, North Carolina, where she is a member of the Peace Haven Writer's Group. She has been writing poetry since the 1960's. Some of her poems were showcased in the Meriden Record Journal in Connecticut when she was a resident there and a member of the Pennons of Pegasus Poetry Group. Currently she writes stories from her life as a collection of family history.

Cuba Revisited

by Beth Bixby Davis

On a beautiful April day in Havana, Bix marveled as she stood in Revolutionary Square looking at the office of Raul Castro. The surrounding buildings displayed oversized, stainless steel cutouts of the heads of Che Guevara, the most-revered revolutionary hero, and former president, Fidel Castro. A towering monument included a large statue of José Marti, an exiled national hero loved for his poetry and prose. Our new luxury Chinese tour bus, parked at the side, stood in stark contrast to the lines of colorful vintage American cars from the 1950s and early 1960s. In that moment a clear memory flooded her mind from more than 50 years earlier in New York City.

It was October 22, 1962, when Bix and other students on the North Wing of Maxwell Hall were gathered in their friend Bertsch's dorm room around her tiny black and white TV. Bertsch was the only student with a television. President John F. Kennedy was preparing to speak about the Cuban missile crisis. For 13 days the United States and the Soviet Union had confronted each other.

The U.S. had failed earlier, in April 1961, to overthrow the Castro regime in Cuba by supporting Cuban refugees from America invading at the Bay of Pigs. Therefore, early in 1962, Soviet premier Nikita Khrushchev and Cuba's revolutionary leader Fidel Castro had reached a secret agreement to place Soviet nuclear missiles in Cuba to deter future attempts at invasion.

These young students were fearful – living in New York City – that they sat in the bulls-eye if this tension escalated into a nuclear war. They had listened to bits and pieces of the news, hoping for a peaceful resolution. To make matters worse, Bertsch's fiancé was a U.S. Marine deployed to Cuba at the time. She had not heard from him in several weeks. She only knew that he was assigned to help guard the U.S. base at Guantanamo Bay.

The October 22nd address by the president came when reassurances by a trusted leader were much needed. A tired-looking president looked directly into the camera and began to speak. No sound was made in that dorm room. The president related that an American spy plane had secretly photographed nuclear missile sites being built on Cuba by the Soviet Union. He quietly and calmly described the situation. He announced a blockade had been put in place to prevent further movement of supplies to Cuba. He demanded removal of the missiles. The students remained concerned.

Bix's mind floated back to the present from that distant memory. Here she was in Cuba, our mysterious island neighbor about which we know so little. A long and unfortunate embargo imposed by the U.S. for half a century had severely limited trade and tourism to this lovely country, but now that had changed. She had come to see for herself as part of a people-to-people travel exchange.

What a contrast she experienced from being a terrified student 50 years ago to a retired adult traveling to Cuba. An invitation into the home of Lorenzo, a well-respected artist and photographer inspired her and lifted her appreciation of Cuban arts. She rode through Havana with Mandy in his purple '56 Ford convertible hearing of his family's decades-long pride in it. Eating delicious food in small family restaurants called paladares and meeting the relatives who ran them was such a treat. She learned more than she could have imagined from Jorge, her brilliant Cuban guide with double PhDs.

A visit to the Havana Club to enjoy a revival of pre-Revolutionary Cuban music performed by world-famous Buena Vista Social Club was an opportunity of a lifetime. Bix toured a cigar factory and talked with workers. Despite the extreme poverty, the Cuban people she met seemed healthy and content. They have good, free health care, free education and everyone has a job, but that might be misleading. She talked at length with an accomplished pianist who is paid the equivalent of $20 a month.

What an education we experienced on this people-to-people exchange. Cuba still has problems, but the people we met there were a wonderful, talented, kind, contented and welcoming people. Even though they have little in material wealth, their basic needs are met and, so far, have not been exposed to the

Cuba Revisited

103

high-tech, high-speed hassle that distresses so many Americans in the U.S. They were openly proud of their country, culture and customs and so willing to share about them. They were very curious and interested in our country and culture. Our driver, Yuri, wore a cowboy hat and dreams of someday visiting Texas.

People are people the world over, generally good, friendly, and accepting of each other. It's the politicians who create the friction and threaten wars. •

Beth Bixby Davis was born in Northern New York and moved to the Asheville area of North Carolina in the mid-1960s where she reared her family, raised Arabian horses and had a 30-year career in nursing. Enjoying a long-time hobby of writing essays and poetry, she recently has taken classes in flash fiction and poetry writing. She belongs to Talespinners Writers Group.

The Call of the Forest
by Bohdan Dziadyk

You've got to start somewhere, and in my case, Daniel Boone made me do it.

In the 4th grade we students had the opportunity to purchase inexpensive books on various topics. My brother, Walt, and I both wanted the book on "Cowboys and Indians," but he, being two years older, got first choice. I settled for the other book we discussed, something about a famous frontiersman. I don't remember the title, but I've never forgotten the first line: "Daniel Boone was born and grew up in a land that was wild and dangerous." It was my first personal book and it took me two weeks to read, but its call was irresistible.

A year later my friends and I all got BB guns for Christmas, but I soon wanted something more. Because we were too young for firearms, I decided to make one. How to do that? Enter the "firecracker gun." I reasoned that an exploding firecracker could be used to launch a projectile through a tube. Sometime later while fishing with my father on the Mississippi River, I found a plank of drift lumber that fitted my new scheme well enough.

The plan was to make a "muzzle loader" with just the essentials: a lock, a stock and a barrel. I sawed and sanded the plank to proper shape, cut a groove and attached a brass barrel, and designed my own firing mechanism—the gun lock—from scratch. A flintlock was impossible, but a "cap lock," of sorts, seemed plausible. A drilled, steel bolt fastened to the side of the stock would receive the fuse from the fire-cracker in the barrel. The hardest part was making and fitting an S-shaped hammer that would interact with a bent nail trigger. A removable piece of oak served as a breech block which sealed the back end of the barrel when firing. A single cap (from a roll of caps for a cap pistol) placed on the bolt nipple would be struck by the spring-powered hammer, shooting a spark onto the fuse for ignition.

This thing was as practical as a screen door on a submarine, but I felt good that in three days I had conceived the idea, gathered the materials and hand tools, and constructed a shootable black-powder gun. When I prepared everything just so, it really worked. Pop, "hiss-s-s-s," bang it went, and the pebble I had loaded down the muzzle shot out with consider-able force. Because the explosions battered the breech block, the mechanism failed after about two dozen shots, but I was satisfied with what I had learned.

In a day without cell phones or portable electronics of any sort, these are the interests that absorbed us. As poor immigrant kids, Walt and I, along with our companions, spent long days in the wilderness as we learned to identify trees and edible plants, to catch pan fish in the creeks, to hunt small game in the forest, to make a fire in the wet woods, and to camp for days at a time with only such skills. And as we did so, we grew into responsible adults, avoiding many problems plaguing students today.

Nearing high school graduation, I faced the question, what next. I had three choices: get a factory job such as Dad and most of the local men had, enter the military as my brother and some friends had done, or go to college. Well, I became a first generation college student and graduated from Southern Illinois University in four years with a Bachelor of Arts degree in biology. I found I really liked the academic setting, so, before entering the military, I was accepted into a master's program. After completing military service and seven years in graduate school I became a professor in a liberal arts college. That suited me well, so I remained for a 36-year career combining teaching with research at biological field stations.

The old saying, "You can take a boy out of the woods, but you can't take the woods out of the boy," summarizes my life journey. I will soon become the proud owner of a custom-made flintlock rifle by gun maker *extraordinaire* Lowell Haarer of Virginia. I met Lowell at the Contemporary Longrifle Association annual show in Lexington, Kentucky, and was impressed by the man and his craftsmanship. I ordered one of his "nothing fancy" guns to bring my journey full circle. I trust this product of his years-wrought expertise will work better and last longer than the firecracker gun made by an American boy as he discovered a new world. •

After serving in the U.S. Army for three years as a Special Forces medic, Bohdan Dziadyk completed M.S. and Ph.D. degrees in botany and ecology. For 36 years, he was a professor of biology at Augustana College in Rock Island, Illinois. Since retiring in 2016, he has maintained his interests in environmental studies and natural history.

Discovery on an Old Country Road
by Marcia Phillips

D iscovering history does not necessarily mean finding the unknown. It often is uncovering depths of stories already known. Such was the case for me concerning three men represented by historic markers on U.S. Highway 64 in Davie County, North Carolina. As significant as the markers are, they tell cold hard facts cast in metal, reducing human drama to something steely. They state that Daniel Boone's family had farmed along the banks of Bear Creek, on the same land that abolitionist Hinton Helper was born and raised, down the road from the farm Tom Ferebee left to become the bombardier on the *Enola Gay*. Three young men from three miles on this old winding road and from three different centuries changed history in three very different ways. Was that just coincidence or was there something about the place that nurtured their spirits of adventure and courage to make their mark? As vastly different as were their paths in life, what did they have in common? I discovered more to this story than the markers told.

My trek of discovery was far from the wooded paths that Boone tramped down finding his way through the Cumberland

Gap in 1769. My path took me from climbing in the remote cave his family was said to shelter in briefly to deciphering faded handwriting in archived books to the technology of internet searching. But I found adventurers who had much in common. Boone, Helper and Ferebee all hunted and fished on the banks of Bear Creek and in the process developed the skills that would lead them on their own paths of discovery, one with his hand on a musket, another with a pen in hand and the third with his hand on a lever that would introduce atomic warfare to the world. Also in common, I learned, was the independent spirit that compelled each to find his way to contribute to history. When I compared the only extant likeness of Daniel Boone, painted when he was 85-years-old, and the school photo of Tom Ferebee in overalls, striking was the similarity in their eyes——both had the piercing intensity of wanderlust. It was as if they were looking beyond the constraints of their humble surroundings to another place. No historic marker can capture that.

Along the way I discovered the still unanswered secrets of a mysterious Frenchman who showed up in Davie County, literally, claiming to have been Napoleon Bonaparte's right-hand man. Having escaped execution in France, he taught a generation of Carolina farm boys how to fence and play the flute. The answers to his mystery lie buried in a grave on a quiet local hillside and in a missing document hidden in some faraway place, yet to be discovered.

Researching their stories meant studying the remnants their lives had left behind in varied forms. Their footprints in the muddy creekbank where they fished long ago have been obliterated, but they left their marks in other obscure ways. Only Boone wrote an autobiography, which disappeared down a river when his canoe overturned. Helper's incidental references to his family were in a conflicted context and Ferebee's controversial actions restrained him until a few late-in-life interviews. Remarkably, all these men lived dangerous lives but survived into old age, giving more clues to find. Other relics such as the Boone cabin stood until the 20th century when it fell victim to progress. I found myself limited, as all historians are, to what survives water, fire, and humans who most destroy, neglect or otherwise impact the existing record. Historical artifacts move around with those who carry them with them so research has to follow their paths. The fine tradition of historians is to bring together the bits of the story and then bring it to life. So it was, I wrote *Davie County Mavericks, Four Men Who Changed History* as a labor of love for the community which nurtured these lives.

Remarkable patterns emerged in my research, in ways unseen until the dots are connected. None of their lives overlapped. Ironically, nine years separated these men's lifespans every time. They could not have known each other; moreover, I found no evidence the later ones were impacted by any knowledge of their forerunners (as I would have liked, so research can disappoint as well as deliver). It was as if the same gap of time punctuated the different eras of these independent maverick lives. The bigger picture often helps make sense of the smaller ones.

Reconstructing history is a process of discovery, tracking old stories to create new paths of understanding and inspiration.

Discovery on an Old Country Road

Thanks to Misters Boone, Helper, Ney, and Ferebee and the trails they left, I was able to make that journey and take others along down an old country road. •

Copyright 2019, Marcia Phillips

Historian Marcia Phillips, who grew up and lives in Davie County, is the author of the award-winning book *Davie County Mavericks, Four Men Who Changed History* published by The History Press in 2018. After teaching history and working in the museum field for many years, she is now the Executive Director of the Advocacy Center of Davie Center. Discovering history and telling the story is her passion and pastime.

The Brown-Sign Challenge
by Gretchen Griffith

During our traveling days, my family became well acquainted with the simple concept of brown signs, the ones along the highway announcing recreational and historical locations open to the public. We were able to spot them readily as we sped down the highway. We were delighted usually, well, maybe just us adults at first—for the driver to veer off course to explore the possibilities, knowing adventure and surprise lay ahead.

Our introduction to these signs started when my husband, Van, and I loaded our two children into a custom conversion van complete with captain's chairs and fold-down bed, for a 9,500-mile, 28-day round-trip drive from Lenoir, North Carolina, to the grand state of Alaska. The year was 1984, a decade before the world wide web arrived in our home, so we accomplished the two years of planning the old-fashioned way. We used an inch-thick trip-tik from "Triple A" showing route suggestions, mail-ordered pamphlets from communities along the route, and one indispensable resource: *Mileposts of the Alaskan Highway.*

At last underway, we explored a world we had only seen in pictures. We were awed by scenic views of a landscape that mere photographs could never do justice. We were amazed by a wide variety of wild creatures close enough to appreciate, yet far enough to keep our 11- and 8-year-old children from daring to approach them. We touched chunks of icebergs which had calved in the recent past and even kept one fragment in the icebox for at least five days.

As spontaneity is the mother of adventure, our trip itinerary often deviated from our original plans as brown signs drew us to unexpected discoveries. We immersed ourselves in curated and interpreted parks and sites. We made rice paper/seaweed rubbings from petroglyphs on the shore. We walked through historical sites preserved from an ancient Native American past and from the pioneer days of the Canadian prairies and the gold rush years of the Yukon.

Because we later shared with excitement about our surprise at the many brown-sign attractions we encountered along the journey, my brother's family countered with a surprise of their own: the "Brown-Sign Challenge." Or as my husband called it, the "What-have-we-gotten-ourselves-into-now? Challenge." It came in the form of a Christmas gift from my brother's family. I opened the fancily wrapped present to find a small, black, National Parks Passport and a two-inch thick guidebook of U.S. National Parks and Historical Sites.

"We challenge you to a duel," my brother proclaimed, showing us his family's identical passport. "Whichever family accumulates the most passport stamps this year will be the winner;

and, the losing family must treat the other to a meal."

"Challenge accepted!" we resoundingly declared, even knowing our Alaska trip visits would not count.

We spent our cold, winter days charting routes that offered the most brown-sign sites per trip. The National Park Guidebook became our constant resource in those pre-internet days. By the time the spring thaw arrived, we were ready. Our first passport stamp came from a Saturday trip to the Revolutionary War site at Kings Mountain National Military Park just south of the North Carolina/South Carolina line. From there we traveled throughout the Southern states seeking out battle-grounds and birth places, which seemed to be most inconveniently miles away from the major highways. We introduced the historically accurate Daniel Boone and Davy Crockett to our children and we gained new perspectives on many previously obscure historical figures.

Soon enough, life got in the way and we were tied down with our son's sports-team schedules and our daughter's teenage activities. When Christmas rolled around, we lagged far behind my brother's family, so we requested a year's extension. After all, we reasoned, the challenge was a little skewed in their favor as they lived in eastern Pennsylvania with an overabundance of brown signs in surrounding states. In actuality, we never did end the challenge or declare a winner by counting stamps. None of us wanted to finish this quest. And that's a good thing.

The end goal might have been bragging rights, but the real goal was instilling in our children a spirit of adventure and exploration, along with a lot of pride in our American history. In our age of modern technology, the "Brown-Sign Challenge" continues within our family. I know this because of texts from my daughter-in-law reporting proudly on behalf of their children: "We're stopping at a brown sign!"

My husband and I recently celebrated our 50th wedding anniversary. Our son's family presented us with a special gift we greatly treasure: a huge, brown sign in the tradition of those road signs we so long pursued. It read:

"Van and Gretchen

Est. 1968." •

Copyright 2019, Gretchen Griffith

Gretchen Griffith has been instrumental in preserving North Carolina mountain stories through oral history projects resulting in several narrative nonfiction books. Her collection of interviews is on file in the Gamewell town hall. She is a former teacher and the author of children's picture books. She lives in Lenoir with her husband, frequently visiting her son's family in Gastonia and infrequently her daughter's in Colorado. Contact her at www.gretchengriffith.com.

A Place I Can Still Find
by Chris Helvey

When we think of going exploring, our thoughts typically turn to preparing for some rugged adventure—getting our passports and vaccinations, hiring a guide and maybe porters, buying our tents, sleeping bags, and dehydrated food. But a journey of exploration doesn't have to be one we are going to make to the Serengeti, Antarctica, or Machu Picchu. It can be an exploration of a nearby woods, a state park we've never seen, or a city we've heard about for years but never visited. In my case, it was a trip to a place connected to a warm, inviting past.

One of the highlights of my 1950s Missouri childhood was a visit each summer to my maternal grandparents' farm. Located north of Kansas City in Platte County, the farm lay on the north side of Highway H that ran from New Market to Weston. My entire family would travel there each year after school let out in Crane, where my father was Superintendent of Schools. I still vividly recall how eagerly I looked forward to "going to the farm" and how excited I got when we turned on H (it's paved now, but in those days was a gravel road).

Time, of course, has continued as part of the journey, too. My grandparents are long dead and the farm sold. I've moved on myself—first to Arkansas, then to Kentucky. Memories of the farm and those halcyon, summer days of my youth gradually faded with the miles and years. However, memory is a strange and wonderful creature and my thoughts recently returned to the farm with such regularity that I soon felt compelled to make a return visit, to see if I could find the farm I so vividly remembered.

Getting to New Market from my current home in Frankfort, Kentucky, wasn't much of a challenge. It's basically an interstate ride all the way. But after I turned off I-29, I began to sense I was making two journeys in one—a trip to Platte County, Missouri, and a trip back in time.

The white, frame Christian Church in New Market evoked memories of attending an old-fashioned ice cream social there with my grandfather, probably around 1959. Then I recalled my mother sharing that in her childhood (she was born in 1927) she knew a very old lady who, as a girl, had actually seen a gathering of Platte County boys ride off to join the Confederacy.

The State of Missouri does a fine job with its signage these days and I found Highway H with no trouble. Going by memory, I turned west and began to roll in the hills, across Bee Creek, past Judge Pepper's old place. I drove up a slope and there it was—the turnoff to my grandparents' farm.

The gravel drive was shorter than I recalled and the front pastures that once held sheep were now mown until they were like lawns. The white picket fence, the ramshackle wooden garage, and the hen house were all gone, but the frame house still stood and I could see the old barn down in the swale. A station wagon sat under a maple tree in the side yard, so I screwed up my courage and walked around to the back door and knocked.

As I waited for someone to come to the door, I wondered how much the old farmhouse had changed. Would I find a house so different on the inside that I would not know it, or …

Then the door swung open and a pleasant, middle-aged face smiled at me. She greeted me with "Yes?" I quickly explained why I had appeared suddenly on her doorstep and asked politely if I could take a quick tour of the old house. She welcomed me and I stepped inside, a bit anxious at what I would find.

I found the interior of my grandparents' home much the same as I remembered. The same built-in, glass-front, curio cabinets were there. The wood and oil stove in what I always called the parlor remained. The view out the kitchen window still revealed the roof of the D.C. Lamar place, and the smooth wooden stairs still led to the bedroom my mother had occupied as a Depression-Era farm girl.

So, I can't claim to have climbed rugged peaks, stalked ferocious wildlife, or shot white-water rapids, but I did make a personal journey that brought back memories long covered

A Place I Can Still Find

over by years of living. I explored my own past and reconnected with ancestors—in my mind at least—who have moved on to the next world in body, but whose spirits, thankfully, still linger in a place I can still find. •

Chris Helvey lives in Frankfort, Kentucky. His short stories have appeared in numerous reviews and journals, including *Kudzu*, *The Chaffin Journal*, *Best New Writing*, *New Southerner*, *Bayou*, *Dos Passos Review*, and *Coal City Review*. His novel, *Whose Name I Did Not Know*, and his short story collection, *Claw Hammer*, are both available from Hopewell Publications. His latest novel, *Snapshot*, was recently released by Livingston Press. Helvey currently serves as the Editor-in-Chief of *Trajectory Journal*.

Aerial Adventure

by Suzanne Cottrell

"Ready?" Debbie's voice quivered.

"I guess so."

Could two 65-year-old women in moderate physical condition have the strength and stamina to tackle 42 obstacles high above the ground? Despite my fear of heights, I envisioned myself hopping from obstacle to obstacle like an agile squirrel.

My best friend, Debbie, and I donned our gear—helmets, gloves, and harnesses—with the hope of completing the tree-top obstacle course. My eyes widened as I read a sign: "Highest platform - 41 feet, Longest Zip Line - 516 feet." My heart beat quickened. I bit my lip. *What was I thinking?*

Our guide led us to a zip line practice area for a safety procedures orientation.

"You go first," nudged Debbie. "This was your idea."

"You're up," signaled our guide. "Remember to start running in the air as you approach the landing ramp."

Sounds easy. I climbed to the wooden platform and attached my two safety cables. *I can do this.* I squinted as the breeze brushed back my hair. I sped down the zip line faster than my legs could pump. My body turned backwards, and I dragged my heels in the sawdust. My cheeks flushed. *He had made it sound so easy.*

"Okay, your turn to show me up."

"Don't count on it," replied Debbie. She replicated my landing.

With our brief training completed, we launched ourselves onto our series of challenging obstacles. Ascending a ladder, we faced our first—crossing from platform to platform across and up a rope net. We re-attached our safety-harness cables and walked around the platform hugging the tree. I swung and bounced off the cargo net. I groped for the ropes. My feet kept slipping through the swaying mesh. I clambered across the netting. At last, I planted my feet on the opposite platform, bent over, and gasped. *One obstacle down, 41 more to go.* Encouraged, I scanned the spring canopy of leaves. Sunlight filtering through the tree tops captivated me until a blue jay cawed and startled me. *Are you mocking me?*

"You can do it," I reassured Debbie.

Debbie kept bouncing off the net. She wrapped her arms through the cords. She climbed half way up. "I don't think I can make it."

"Attach this cable to your harness, and I'll hoist you up to the platform," explained the guide below.

"Are you okay?" I asked. "We can stop any time."

"No, way. I'm not giving up."

In our naivete, we tried some challenging obstacles, like traversing dangling metal hoops, which required more balance, agility, and stamina than we could muster. As we tired, we opted for paths of lesser resistance.

I scrutinized each suspended obstacle. I refused to be intimidated by boards, rings, and ropes. My motions were deliberate like a tightrope walker's, I imagined. However, each time I reached a zip line platform, my arms eagerly embraced the tree trunk. I froze.

"I don't think I can do this" I whined. My palms sweated.

"Just step off and enjoy the ride," encouraged Debbie. "Remember, this is an adventure."

I looked down from the platform's edge and saw two squirrels playing tag around the base of an elm tree. They looked so tiny as if I were looking out an airplane window at a miniature world below. My legs wobbled. *Look out, not down.* The panoramic view eased my discomfort, but not enough to make my feet move forward.

"Debbie, if I don't go on the count of three, just push me," I declared. "One, two, three." I closed my eyes and stepped off. I squinted, tucked up my legs, and felt the rush of air as I soared like a bird. I squealed and then giggled with nervous energy. The tree-top perspective and new sense of freedom were exhilarating. As I neared the landing ramp, I forgot to start running in place. My body turned backward; I landed on my posterior and dragged my heels through the sawdust.

Aerial Adventure

"I made it," I shouted. When I reached that last platform, I was relieved, exhausted, and elated. I launched myself into the final zipline run and screamed. I remembered to run this time, but I was so excited I didn't pay complete attention to the approaching ramp. My landing gear malfunctioned, and I twisted my left ankle. I grimaced in pain as I hobbled off, silencing my urge to cry.

From the top of the platform, Debbie yelled, "Are you okay?"

"Yeah," I offered. My muscles trembled; my left ankle throbbed; warmth radiated throughout my body. Despite my awkwardly painful landing, I was gratified by what I had overcome.

I did it! I actually did it. And next time I'm fearing less, enjoying more, and most certainly wearing high-topped boots. •

Suzanne Cottrell, a member of the Granville Writers' Group and North Carolina Writers' Network, lives with her husband and three rescue dogs in Granville County, North Carolina. An outdoor enthusiast and retired teacher, she enjoys reading, writing, knitting, hiking, Pilates, and yoga. Her prose has appeared in numerous journals and anthologies, including *Bearing Up*, *Pop Machine*, *Unwanted Visitors*, *Empty Silos*, *Dragon Poet Review*, *Dual Coast Magazine*, *Parks and Points*, and *Nailpolish Stories*.

"That Little Road"

by John M. Fox, M.D.

I'm a born Kentuckian who grew up in Louisville. I travelled around the world in the Air Force and through various surgical training programs, but I never felt at home until I came back to Kentucky. The warmth in the air, a green so deep it looks slightly blue, the seasonal changes, and the rolling hills just feel right. I can see what attracted Daniel Boone to the region.

I'm not descended from Daniel Boone, but when I moved to Lexington to set up a medical practice, I was drawn to the side of the town which was on Boone Creek, on Athens-Boonesboro Road, and a mile from Boone Station where the famous pioneer lived for four years. My Louisville childhood neighborhood was next to Cherokee Park, where a statue of Daniel Boone carrying a rifle had stood since 1906. I actually climbed on it back in my day. So, I do indeed have some connection to "Boone."

I remember vaguely hearing of Boone Trace as an original Daniel Boone trail. I also own a motorcycle, so I thought I would combine these two interests and explore the Trace on the bike. I set out in 2009 to see what the Trace was all about. I thought most likely it was just US Highways 25 and 25E.

At the Cumberland Gap National Historical Park near Middlesboro, I spoke to pleasant and well-informed park rangers. I purchased a Kentucky Frontier Trails map created by the University of Kentucky and a book by Randell Jones with the promising title, *In the Footsteps of Daniel Boone*. Those two items then totally screwed up my life with an unrelenting obsession to preserve on the ground what remains of Boone Trace. Thus, began my adventure.

The map was based on research by Neal O. Hammon, a retired architect who researched old surveys and property descriptions in county courthouses along the route looking for references to "Boone Trace."

With the trail map based on Hammon's research, I was able to find remnants of the old trail which was active for thousands of immigrants into Kentucky during about 20 years following its blazing in 1775. I was assisted also by Scott New, another Daniel Boone authority. He kindly spent a couple of hours refining the information of Neal Hammon onto a Kentucky Gazetteer map. This gave me the detail to explore "Boone Trace" on my bike.

This adventure started in 2009, and as I headed down the trail on the bike, it first struck me how pleasant and interesting the route became. Daniel Boone essentially followed buffalo and Indian trails which were tramped out by the big animals who followed the creeks and streams in need of water as they foraged along in search of food and salt licks. He had the knack of connecting these segments if he needed to get from one point to another. Consequently, there is usually a waterway associated with the trail its entire length. After a while, I became familiar with these now-named streams, and they became like old friends.

Soon I began to discover relics and points of interest along the way, and it eventually dawned on me that this trail was really important! Reading up, I found that it was the first road (or trail) into the land that was to become Kentucky. It was important not only to the founding of Kentucky, but to the opening of the entire West. That road—"that little road"—was just that significant and consequential in the history of America. I also found it to be a "spiritual" road where often the faces can be seen and the voices heard of those who came before. And, now it is part of who I am. I wish others to have this same experience.

In time, I realized nobody was doing anything to protect and preserve this route. I remember sitting on the monument in Oakley, Kentucky, in front of the Mount Carmel Church with the bike parked on the road. The monument placed there by the Daughters of the American Revolution in 1915 was rusted and deteriorated. The weathered slab on top of it had "BOON" etched in the stone. Already weary from my all-day ride, I thought, "I can't let this happen. Someone has to do something to save it." For better or worse, my life has not been the same since.

We formed a 501(c)3 non-profit organization with the mission

"That Little Road"

to preserve Boone Trace and to make the American public aware of its historical significance. We called it Friends of Boone Trace. We have completed a master plan in cooperation with the National Park Service and are looking toward the 250th anniversary of the opening of Boone Trace in 2025.

Come join us on the adventure at boonetrace1775.com. Come explore "that little road." •

Dr. John M. Fox is a retired colorectal surgeon from Lexington, Kentucky, where he practiced medicine for 38 years. His interests include athletics, piano, aviation, history, and family. His writing experience has been scant due to these activities except for an occasional "Letter to the Editor," usually rejected for offensive language. His serious love for history only came to life with the trail of Daniel Boone and is now an obsession.

Broken Branch
by Paula Teem Levi

The search for truth is a noble adventure.

A few years ago, my brother, Paul, asked me to help with some family research. Part of our family tree was missing. In the process of breaking through what had been a "brick wall" in our genealogy, an ancestor's life story emerged that would leave a lasting impression on me and other relatives.

I started with only two pieces of information. First, our great-grandmother's death certificate proved her date and place of birth and her parents' names. Second, the 1880 Census placed that Frederick Horton family in Newport, Campbell County, Kentucky, across the Ohio River from Cincinnati. The census showed him as 28 years old with wife, Elizabeth, age 30; son, Jeffrey, age 5; daughter, Priscilla Anne, age 3; and daughter, Ida M., age 1. They were a young and growing family with a string of children about two years apart. From other sources, we know another daughter, Alsonay, was born the day before Halloween, October 30, 1880. That was after the census was taken, so she was not listed. Our mystery was not being able to find this vibrant Horton family in any later census—anywhere.

We took a road trip to Newport to do further research. From an 1882/1883 directory of the town we found at the library, we learned that Fred Horton was employed as a river boss foreman for the George and Botts' Coal Company, retail and wholesale dealers of coal. He probably worked on the river or supervised the movement of coal on barges moving up and down the Ohio.

A search of newspaper records revealed some disconcerting news:

> *The Kentucky State Journal*, Saturday, January 6, 1883. "Fred Horton, of Eglantine Street, river boss for Messrs. George & Botts, is lying low with smallpox and one of his children is dead in the home with the disease. That makes two children and a wife that he has lost since Christmas from the same cause."

That was a startling and sad discovery, and another similarly troubling report came three days later but with a tinge of hope:

> *The Kentucky State Journal*, Tuesday, January 9, 1883. "Fred Horton, who was reported as being dead, is still alive and, although weak, is improving."

Unfortunately, a later story confirmed our worst fears for the fate of our ancestor's family:

> *The Daily Commonwealth*, Thursday, January 11, 1883. "Fred Horton, the superintendent of George and Botts' coal yard, died night before last of smallpox. His

two surviving children are both down with the disease and one of them, yesterday, was in a dying condition. Nearly the entire family is thus swept away, all within a few weeks."

The Statistics of the Newport Cemetery shows that on December 25, 1882, Elizabeth Horton died from smallpox. On December 26, 1882, Annie Horton died from smallpox. On January 6, 1883, Ida Mae Horton died from smallpox. On January 10, 1883, Fred Horton died from smallpox.

Indeed, a smallpox epidemic devastated the Cincinnati region in December 1882 and January 1883. We learned that the bodies of smallpox victims at the Newport Cemetery were placed in a blanket and buried immediately without being placed in a box. The bodies were handled as little as possible. Sometimes the undertaker, with his cart and horse, could not get to all the dead immediately. To prevent the spread of disease, friends and family of the deceased placed the bodies of smallpox victims in a crypt temporarily until they could be buried.

We hoped the two remaining children had survived the smallpox epidemic, Jefferson Davis Horton, the only son, and Alsonay Horton, the youngest daughter. We set out to find them.

Through Ancestry.com I was able to connect with a surviving descendant of Jeff Horton. His great-granddaughter provided valuable information about the fate of the two youngest Horton children. It seems that shortly after Fred's death, Jeff and Alsonay were placed on a coal barge provided by the George and Botts' Coal Company and sent upstream on the Kanawha River to live with relatives in Charleston, West Virginia. Living into their sixties, Jeffrey and Alsonay each died in Charleston in 1945 and 1946 respectively.

The little girl who survived the smallpox epidemic was a great-grandmother to Paul and me. Through our investigative journey, we were able to discover what happened to our ancestors. We now feel as if we somehow traveled with them through their trials and tribulations, their losses. We appreciate the resilience and courage of the two family members who survived smallpox to carry on against other challenges in an unknown future. We now see these family members as actual persons, not just as newly added names completing a broken branch of our family tree. •

Paula Teem Levi lives in Clover, South Carolina. She is a member of several genealogical societies. Breathing life into her ancestors' stories through her writing is her passion. She was involved in the research and writing of a recently published newspaper article about events in World War II. She believes sharing this story may help others break through brick walls they encounter in researching some "broken branches" in their own family trees.

Horse Whispering
for the Average Woman

by Janet Baxter

S ome choices in life substantially alter life's journey. Marriage, children, graduate school may be a few of these forks in our separate paths. The one I didn't expect was riding horses.

"This is not hard," my trainer told me as I fumbled with the rope and my training stick for what seemed the thousandth time. "It's like a dance with your partner." I can't dance.

I rode and just held on for the first few years, riding trails in the North Carolina mountains and piedmont on my Tennessee Walking horses, grinning from ear to ear. We didn't walk; we rode lickety-split, fast and furious. Then I learned a little more about this living, breathing, sports vehicle beneath me and I found the *horse* under me. I learned basic round-pen work, ground manners, and a little about horse behavior. I began to believe I knew something. Much later I took riding lessons.

People in the horse world talk about *feel*, a sense of communication between the horse and the person. I didn't feel a thing.

I concentrated on timing and on learning and experiencing the differences between positive and negative reinforcement. I focused on coordinating cues from my leg, seat, and hands. "Bits are not for braking," I learned; hands and reins are used last, not first. I learned that saddle fit is crucial, and bit size and comfort just as much. I unleashed my enthusiasm and maintained a dogged persistence for learning to do things better. And then I wrenched my knee!

Sometimes I get off my horse while riding and walk for an hour on the trail, combining my exercise with my horse's. One afternoon, while walking with Nugget, my young silver dapple gelding, I stepped on a loose rock, twisting my knee and falling painfully to the ground. Nugget looked down at me as if asking, "and what are you doing down there?" I couldn't get up, couldn't put weight on that leg. I was a mile or maybe two from the parking lot. I sat there waiting for the pain to subside.

A time comes when you have to reach down, find your inner strength, and just do what needs to be done. Luckily this situation was not life-threatening; but, sitting on a trail with your back against a poplar tree at mid-afternoon in early spring and unable to walk out is still daunting. I heard no other riders about; cell phone connection was spotty. It would take hours for the rangers to find me and it would be dark in two or three.

Nugget was still in training. I was not sure how he would handle what I was going to ask him to do. I got up, hopped on my good leg, asked him to be still next to a log. I put all my faith into this young gelding. I asked for a *stand*. He stood.

I held tight to the saddle, put my good foot in the stirrup and raised my hurt leg over his back. As I stretched it, I heard a loud "pop" of the tendon in my knee. Nugget stood still.

"Nugget, we're going to walk back. Let's count cadence." And he stepped off, went carefully through the creek, and walked up the hill. I counted, "One, two, three, four, five, six, seven, eight," to each step—slowly. Nugget stayed under me, stayed in my hand. He carried me to the parking lot and up to friends. This was new for Nugget. My friends helped me dismount— again, new for Nugget—and helped us get home.

One cannot differentiate too much between riding and the rest of one's life. What it takes to train and ride well is also what it takes to lead the life you most want to lead. It includes humility, patience, compassion, assertiveness, and emotional control. It includes a softness in focus, slowing down and staying centered, being mindful in the moment. It means staying with it until the horse gives to your hand, and it takes praise for the slightest try. It means practicing, expecting at times to take one step forward and two steps back. It means understanding the animal's herd culture and communicating with that culture in mind.

A new instructor is helping me continue forward, filling the holes in my horsemanship, building on what I'd learned with much fine tuning. She takes my "can't dance" and is willing to support me on this journey, breaking tasks down into smaller steps for both the horse and me as often as it takes us to get it. I can almost sense that *feel*. •

Horse Whispering for the Average Woman

Janet K. Baxter lives in Kings Mountain, North Carolina, where she is a member of the Kings Mountain Mauney Memorial Library Writer's Group and the Charlotte Writer's Club. Retired as Director of Special Education from the University of North Carolina at Charlotte, her previous writing experience includes winning two city-wide essay contests during high school and publication of professional articles.

Camouflaged Concerns
by Judie Holcomb-Pack

rowing up in Winston-Salem, North Carolina, I seldom drove on snow. At the first mention of snow in a weather forecast, folks stampeded to the grocery stores for milk and bread, then hunkered down until the threat of annihilation by the white fluffy stuff had passed.

Married at 28, I moved with my husband to his hometown of Bristol, Tennessee, from which I made monthly 3-hour trips back home to visit family and friends.

That first November, I left Bristol on a beautiful, warm fall day and dressed accordingly – jeans and a light shirt. As I prepared to head back, the weather was the same with a few wispy clouds in a Carolina-blue sky. When I reached the Blue Ridge Plateau, the sky turned to a dull gray, but I wasn't worried. We don't have bad weather in November. (This was before global climate change became a popular notion.)

At I-81, it was spitting snow—just flurries. Nothing to worry about. I stopped for coffee and once outside was shocked by how much the temperature had dropped. It was cold!

I noticed a beat-up pickup truck with a gun rack and two men dressed in hunter's garb pull out of the parking lot just ahead of me. I paid them little attention. I was focused on driving in what soon became a blinding snow storm. Then the pickup slowed down and let me pass and pulled in behind me. Were they following me?

I crept along the interstate, able to see only three feet ahead. Scared and shaking, I pulled over to what I hoped was the side of the road. I prayed for a highway patrolman to come rescue me. Or Santa Claus!

The pickup pulled over behind me and one of the hunters walked over and knocked on my window. I had read my share of true crime stories, so I inched my window down slightly and kept the door locked and the car in gear. "Do you need any help?" he asked.

Red flag! Stranger danger! I declined his help and suggested instead they drive slowly in front of me and I would follow their tracks.

We started off together, but soon enough I was well outside my comfort zone driving. I pulled over again, and the guy came back to my car.

"Sure you don't want me to drive your car, lady?" he asked again.

I weighed my choices. "Well, if you promise not to rape me and steal my car, I guess it would be okay."

"Lordy, Honey," he said. "What kind of person do you think I am?"

That was the question, I suppose, and I wasn't sure how to answer it. I just knew I had to get home and this was my only option. I had visions of my frozen body being found after the spring thaw.

The fellow got in my car and we headed slowly away from Wytheville. Then I realized my anxiety plus that large cup of coffee was starting to affect me—I had to pee. I asked him to stop at the next rest area so I could call my husband, emphasizing "husband." I wanted hubby to know I was in the hands of total strangers.

"I'm going to the bathroom first," I said. "You're not going to steal my car while I'm gone, are you?"

At this, the fellow laughed, promising me he would be right there when I got back. "Where's your coat?" he asked,

"I don't have a coat. Didn't need one when I left home."

This fellow I was so worried about took off his heavy camouflage jacket and handed it to me to put on. Bundled in it, I tried to call on the pay phone, but all the lines were dead. So off we went again, two guys and a girl wearing a stranger's jacket, trying to get back home.

Hours later when we pulled into Abingdon, Virginia, the snow had let up considerably. I thanked the two fellows profusely, but in my flustered state, I didn't even get their names! But I do remember asking them why they had followed me. They had noticed I was a young woman alone, they said, and my car had North Carolina tags. So, they figured I just might need some help in the impending snow storm.

I had let my imagination run wild and think the worst about two men who were actually good Samaritans on the road to Bristol.

A trip that usually took three hours had taken me over six, but I was safely home, thanks to two angels in camouflage. •

Judie Holcomb-Pack is retired from Winston-Salem's Crisis Control Ministry. She is editor/writer for the Winston-Salem Chronicle and their publication "For Seniors Only" magazine. She won gold medals in Senior Games/SilverArts competitions for poetry and short stories. She serves on the boards of Winston-Salem Writers and 40 Plus Stage Company. Judie enjoys a great cup of coffee and stimulating conversation; and, she is a die-hard Virginia Tech Hokies football fan.

Special Errand
by Deborah Wilson

I remember the weeping willow's branches nearly touching the ground in Momote Village, Japan, where I waited for the bus to arrive. On the cusp of my teenage years, I was waiting for even more to arrive in my life—courage, independence, and self-confidence. Like the tree, I was not a native, but I was cultivated here. The village housed mostly U.S. Air Force families, and a few Army families like my own. With $20 in my wallet—more money than I'd ever had entrusted to me—I was on a special errand. I was growing up.

Tokyo's famous Ginza lay halfway between Momote Village and my destination, Grant Heights. It was in the Ginza that my mother taught me how to shop, to select cucumbers for their size and freshness. I noticed that ripe watermelons would sometimes be yellow inside, instead of red as they are in the United States. Together we selected the white blouses with embroidered collars, the staple of my school wardrobe. My father taught me how to select the right size shoes. I quickly learned that Japanese athletic shoes lasted longer than American-made canvas shoes. The exception to the rule was losing one down the open sewers that lined the narrow back-streets of Tokyo.

A military dependent who shopped both Japanese markets and on military bases, I was comfortable with Japanese and American currency. Ten yen was worth three cents. I could almost work the exchanges in my head.

Having been taught to respect my elders, I never became comfortable with elderly Japanese bowing to me, a mere child. I had to remind myself that Japan was an occupied country. I would return the bow respectfully and continue my business.

The bus arrived and I was on my way, past the "Condition Green" sign marking the Momote Village exit. The bus traveled down the steep, benched hillside until it stopped at the bottom where the road intersected the main highway.

"Bakka!" a driver shouted. A motorcyclist skidded, careening into the bus, and sliding behind the bus's front wheels.

We would have to wait, and I knew exactly what my mother would think when I was late. Buses ran every hour, and I had been riding them independently since receiving my military ID card at age 10. A string of military bases ran across Tokyo. One base lay underground, providing a concrete shelter in case of nuclear disaster, a playground being the only clue to its existence. Another major base was Yokota. The route ended at Tachikawa AFB where newcomers landed and those leaving departed for the States. Learning the hard way, I had gotten on a bus that ran the loop in the opposite direction once. It had taken well more than an hour. So, now I was pretty sure my mother would think I was on another misadventure.

Eventually, the police came, checked the injured motorcyclist, and we were able to continue to Grant Heights. That's where three of my brothers had graduated from Narimasu High School. Go Dragons! It was also where the dispensary, chapel, and library were located. I headed directly to the Base Exchange on the first part of my errand, to purchase the 10-cup rice cooker on sale for $10. Next, I went to the Annex to buy brown leather shoes for school. When my feet were measured, I discovered I no longer wore children's shoes. As a 12-year-old heading into seventh grade, I now wore women's shoes. I found a pair that would be comfortable all day, including walking and playing tether ball before school.

I had just enough time to treat myself at the snack bar before catching the last bus home. I enjoyed my usual hamburger, fries, and small cola. I had the electric rice cooker for which I had been sent, new shoes, and change to give my mother.

1964 was a time of change in Tokyo, Japan. Traffic signs written in Japanese and English were being converted to international signs in preparation for the upcoming Olympics. It would be the first Olympics televised via satellite to the rest of the world, and Olympic flags were everywhere. Even coinage sported Olympic rings. I lived in the middle of a world that was changing, just as I was.

At summer's end, I returned to the World War II barracks at Camp Drake that served as the junior high school. The school nurse did a double-take, seeing how much I had grown over the summer. My confidence was further boosted when the physical-education teacher said, "Some of the most feminine women in the world are athletes." Having also proved myself worthy of my mother's trust, I accepted I was no longer a little girl. •

Born in front of her grandmother's Texas home, Deborah C. Wilson is the seventh of nine children. Like everybody in her mostly military family, she has traveled. She takes inspiration from her adventures. Deborah now lives in Winston-Salem, North Carolina, and is a member of Winston-Salem Writers. Her story "Earning the Badge" appeared in *Bearing Up*, the results of the Personal Essay Publishing Project winter 2018.

The Virginia Beauty
and My "Johnny Appleseed"
by Karen Jones Hall

American folklore is full of stories including Paul Bunyan and Johnny Appleseed. Unlike the fantastical Paul Bunyan and his blue ox, Babe, however, the Johnny Appleseed story is based on a real man, John Chapman, whose life was far more interesting than his legend.

Chapman grew up during the Revolutionary War in Massachusetts and set out as a missionary preaching a rather unusual religion across the expanding American frontier. Unlike his legend, however, John Chapman was not simply wandering across America's landscape, planting apple trees willy-nilly during the late 18th and early 19th centuries. Instead, he was planting orchards to acquire land as a homesteader under the laws which encouraged people to occupy the former Indian lands declared open to settlement. Once the trees were bearing fruit, he would sell the land and turn a tidy profit. He also established nurseries and sold the apple trees themselves to farmers. His doing this across Pennsylvania, Ohio, Indiana, and Illinois gave birth to the legend of an American farmer completely enthralled by apples. Well, my family has its own "Johnny Appleseed."

Martin Dickerson Stoneman was the son of a first-generation American, a Quaker, John Stoneman and his wife, Elizabeth Hickman Stoneman. He was my 3rd great-grandfather. Martin lived in the generation after John Chapman, but he still had a meaningful impact on the American apple industry. His legend lives on today as a cultivator of the "Virginia Beauty," a delicious, soft, red apple found in Virginia.

Martin Stoneman's apple legend began around 1850 when he stumbled upon this scrumptious apple. Family lore says he was at a family reunion with his children and grandchildren in a little place called Gambetta, Virginia, located in Carroll County (formerly Grayson County) on the New River. During this family feast, family members noted that Martin gorged himself on the plentiful spread of food and then excused himself home. The grandchildren were so worried, they followed him home. Along the way they found Grandpa Martin sitting under an apple tree with a pile of spotted red apples piled up between his legs and his pocket knife in hand cutting out the bad spots. He was just "pigging out" again. Martin became a family legend for being a bottomless pit for that tasty, brick-red apple.

From his discovery, Martin began grafting this apple tree on his farm. The discovered tree was located on the farm of a neighbor, Zachariah Safewright. It had begun bearing fruit around 1826. In this small community of miners and farmers, that apple was known locally as "Zach" or "Zach Red."

Around 1850 Martin renamed this apple the "Virginia Beauty." Just a few years after the Civil War ended, Martin had enough grafted trees to begin selling the apples.

Unlike Martin's Virginia Beauty, John Chapman's apples were not for eating. His were for making cider and applejack. They were "smack your momma" tart! Water was unsafe to drink in many places due to bacteria, but cider was safe due to fermentation occurring during the distillation process. It produced bacteria-killing alcohol. So, technically these brewers were making hard cider. During Prohibition, laws made it illegal to make this cider, so many of Chapman's trees were cut down by axe-wielding "revenuers" and G-men in the 1920's. This nearly killed America's connection to hard cider.

Chapman preferred planting seeds to grafting, but with seeds, no one ever knew what type of apple would spring up. That's just a fact of apple seeds. Martin preferred grafting even though it was a difficult art to master. And, Martin's legend grew with his grafting success.

He began selling his grafted trees to neighboring communities including Galax, Independence, Hillsville, Wytheville, Pulaski, all in Virginia. His apple trees extended into some of the mountain communities in North Carolina including Mount Airy, Sparta, and Wilkesboro as well.

A few years after the Civil War, the Franklin Davis Nursery in Richmond, Virginia, began commercial sales of the Virginia Beauty, advertising the many outstanding qualities of this delicious apple. The soils and the climate of these communities allowed the Virginia Beauty to thrive and produce. With this wide distribution, Martin Dickerson Stoneman became a local "Johnny Appleseed" legend. But, about this same time the Red Delicious apple was discovered in Iowa and grew quickly in popularity. Sadly, the Virginia Beauty was pushed aside as the commercial demand for the Red Delicious overtook it. Consumers were buying their fruit based on its appearance, not its taste. The Red Delicious looked particularly attractive to shoppers although not a particularly sweet apple.

Martin Dickerson Stoneman is a legend in the Stoneman family. He was a farmer beloved in the apple growing industry for discovering the Virginia Beauty. And, dear Grandpa Martin is my "Johnny Appleseed." •

Karen Lynn Jones Hall, currently of Colfax, North Carolina, is an award-winning author of several books about community history in western North Carolina and southwest Virginia. She received awards from the North Carolina Society of Historians for three books: *The Blue Ridge Parkway*, *Building the Blue Ridge Parkway*, and *Granite: Once & Forever*. She has a B.A. in Management and Ethics from John Wesley College and a B.A. in Chemistry from Salem College. She rejoices in family stories.

The Flat Rock Place
Where I Met Daniel Boone
by Joe Brown

I n 1752 Daniel Boone was walking, stalking, hunting, and fishing on the banks of the Yadkin River where I grew up. I was born 200 years later in 1952, and now the paths along those riverbanks connect our lives across all those many years.

When I was 6 years old our family bought a 13-acre farm on Riverview Road in Davie County. It was a couple of miles upstream from the mouth of Dutchman's Creek and only a few miles upstream from a place known as Boone's Cave. With only a dozen or so neighbors in an area covering over 1,000 acres, it was paradise and a great place to grow up.

At first, the small stream flowing a hundred yards behind our house was a training ground for me and my little brother Carl. He was four years younger than I. Exploring there prepared us for the day we would get to prospect the riches of the larger Yadkin River. We practiced fishing and trapping there. By the time I was 13 and 14 and my brother Carl was 9 and 10, we had earned the privilege to spend our recreational time exploring the riverbanks. With trap and reel we became proficient in harvesting fin and fur. I jokingly tell people that Mom was afraid that I would get hurt on a bicycle, so she let me take the old 20-gauge shotgun and go hunting, But it's really true! (I never did get a bicycle, nor did I really want one). For all the years we lived there no deer, no turkeys, and especially no bears, called that neck of the woods home. I know that deer and turkey are back now, and it wouldn't surprise me if bear were moving back in, too. Bears, like people, follow rivers.

Down river from where we kept our homemade wooden boat tied to a tree, a huge rock outcrop came all the way to the water's edge. As you got close to it while going down the river bank path, you would come to a set of natural rock steps that led down to a room-size flat area at the head of the rocks. The place just called out, "Build a fire and stay here tonight." We did just that many times. Even when not fishing or camping there, I would linger at that spot to admire the uniqueness of the "Flat Rock Place." Standing there I would take in the changes in the river's attitude. Sometimes in late summer, if it had been dry, it would be low and almost clear. If it had rained much, it would be reddish to dark red according to the amount of the rains. If it were a long cold spell, you could judge the severity of the temperature by how much ice was on the river.

To leave this Flat Rock Place, you had two choices: back up the stone steps, or if you wanted to go on downstream, a narrow rock ledge that went around the face of the rocks. This rock ledge was only 6-8 inches wide where your feet went. The upper rock tilted away from the water so you can lean into it. I used that downstream path so much that I even knew which foot to lead with to assure a better footing. Even in the dark I could navigate this trail as slick as a whistle. As tricky as it seemed to go that way, it was the only good way to go down-river. It was here I crossed paths with Daniel Boone, even if it has taken me half a century to realize it.

While learning to trap I learned that to successfully catch any critter you had to get it to step on a spot not more than two - inches in diameter. Of all the places in the world he could put his foot, it had to be on that "spot." You had to use a lure—meat, fish, or a special place it wanted to be.

This Flat Rock Place was the lure for humans. In my mind, I know Indians would most surely have liked it, and Daniel Boone would have liked it just as much as I always have.

I've read a few books about Daniel Boone; and, while reading those pages, I could envision the master woodsman coming around that thin foot path curving past the rocks, with his flintlock, Tick Licker, laying in the crook of his arm. I can imagine him carefully placing his feet in the exact spots where I had put mine so many years later.

That Flat Rock Place and my boyhood recollections are where I indeed met Daniel Boone. •

Joseph Brown is a native of North Carolina, born in Yadkin County and raised in Davie County. He now resides in the Bethania area of

The Flat Rock Place Where I Met Daniel Boone

Forsyth County and has lived all his life within 40 miles of his birth-place. Most of his previous writing has been daily journals on his mission trips to Kentucky, Canada, and Ecuador. He still loves all outdoor adventures.

Making Yellow Sparks over the Bluegrass

by Charles H. Bogart

L ots of people love reading history, the complete and distilled story compiled as if it were common knowledge. But some of us enjoy and prefer the challenge of putting those stories together, searching the archives, tracking down the obscure and rumored artifact, and talking to people who know more than we do. That's my passion. It's my challenge and my reward.

In 2001, I set off on a journey of discovery within Kentucky, but I soon found myself farther afield. I was gathering information for a proposed book on the streetcar, trolley, and interurban rail companies of Kentucky. (We insiders call these "traction" operations.) Along the way, I met a fascinating group of people, visited places seldom seen by the average citizen, and gazed upon documents and artifacts not viewed in over a hundred years. I found the unexpected and experienced fair shares of jubilation and disappointment.

A visit to Transylvania College Library's archives brought disappointment to me as the file marked "KT&T" (Kentucky

Traction and Terminal) contained no hidden gems. But for some reason, I picked up a file on the building of US Highway 27 south from Lexington to Nicholasville. Eureka! The photos were not of building US 27 but, instead, were of the construction of the right-of-way of the interurban rail line between those two cities. Great serendipity and my good fortune.

Hearing of an upcoming railroad artifact show in Columbus, Ohio, I drove there from Frankfort, Kentucky. At the show, I found for sale a box of streetcar photographs. The photos were from all over the United States, sort of a grab-bag, and so the price was right. After getting back home, I began to examine each photo. Among the photos was one which surprised and thrilled me. It was a photo of some folks watching the running of the last streetcar in Kentucky. That happened in Ft. Mitchell. One of the watchers was my younger father-in-law standing in front of his house. And as amazing as that might seem, holding his hand was a little girl, five years old, my future wife. What a find! What a treasure.

A number of people had told me a number of times I should definitely meet with a gentleman who lived in Knoxville, Tennessee. He had a collection of streetcar memorabilia, they said, so I drove to his house. His collection of streetcar memorabilia was indeed amazing and he gladly shared information with me. But what was more impressive was in his backyard. He had built a 1:7-scale electric trolley line behind his house. Not only did I get to ride on this trolley, but I also got to operate it. Great fun.

Throughout my search for material for my book, I kept

hearing the story of Elmer Sulzer's lost manuscript. Sulzer was the author of *Ghost Railroads of Kentucky*. I'd heard he had also started a book on the abandoned interurban lines in Kentucky. The common theme of these stories was that Sulzer had finished the manuscript and had sent it out for review among various traction raconteurs just before he died. A number of people commented on having read the manuscript but no one knew where it was. This tale sounded to me like the Appalachian tale of Johnathan Swift's Silver Mine. But, again by luck and perseverance, I found a carbon copy of one of the chapters of this proposed book in the Kentucky Room at the Shelbyville Library. Mystery solved.

But not every opportunity for discovery ended positively My research led me to the painting Sulzer had commissioned for use on the cover of his planned book, "Ghost Interurban Lines of Kentucky." The painting was of a KT&T Cincinnati Curveside car running alongside Paris Pike. It was an attractive picture at a reasonable price, but the bottom 6-inches of the 3-foot painting was water-stained. When I finally talked myself into purchasing the painting, I was too late. Someone else had snatched it up.

In 2011, I published my book, *Yellow Sparks Over the Bluegrass.* I borrowed that interesting title from a local historian's description of his ride on the Kentucky Traction & Terminal (KT&T) interurban rail between Lexington and Paris during a snow storm. Those words resonated with me and seemed to describe as much my energized experience of pulling together the facts for this historical account.

Discoveries and adventures come in all shapes and sizes. It all depends on what we like to explore and why. What sparks your interest—yellow or otherwise? •

Charles H. Bogart graduated from Thomas More College with a BA in History. He lives in Frankfort, Kentucky, where he is a docent at the Fort Boone Civil War Battle Site and a Conductor at the Bluegrass Railroad Museum. He has authored a number of books and articles on railroad, Civil War, and Western River history. He is president of the CSXT Historical Society and the Frankfort Civil War Roundtable.

For What I Knew Was Right

by Bill Gramley

It was 1966 and I was 32, had a wife and four children, and was then the pastor of a Moravian church on the outskirts of Winston-Salem, North Carolina.

In 1967, a minister friend of mine said, "Bill, why don't you go to Washington and find out what this war in Vietnam is all about?" So, I arranged to ride to Washington, D.C., with a couple of Quakers. We went, we listened, we learned. And what we learned was that the war—then involving American troops, helicopters, and planes in ever-increasing numbers since 1965—was actually a civil war between North Vietnam and South Vietnam. Ho Chi Minh of the North had declared independence from Japan and then fought off the French, their longtime colonial rulers, defeating them at Dien Bien Phu in 1954. The French left, but people in the South did not like the Communist government of North Vietnam and asked the United States to come and help them.

When I came back from Washington, I was convinced that we were really no different from the French colonialists and were messing in a civil war like other imperialists.

I didn't know everything about the fighting, but I did believe that this war was wrong and that the death and destruction was a waste of human life. While some leaders in our nation could see that this was a losing battle in which we were getting bogged down, the fear of Communism's spread was enough to override their questions and challenges. And yet, we soon learned we were propping up a corrupt dictator in Saigon. And the lies our government told about body counts added to my unrest.

I began to write letters to the editors of the *Winston-Salem Journal* and *Twin City Sentinel*. I began to preach against the war. I remember one sermon entitled "Wake Up and Die Right." In it, I pointed out how this war was getting more and more inhumane, was killing civilians, and was causing atrocities. Stories were coming out about our troops throwing prisoners out of helicopters and flame throwers burning down villages. It was mostly the killing and the lies from Washington I protested.

I still clearly remember one time when I was working with a few others in Winston-Salem for an effort called "Negotiation Now." I was standing silently on the post office steps on Fifth Street holding a sign to that effect when a couple from my church drove by. They looked at me and surely wondered what in the world their pastor was doing. Around that time, some members went behind my back to petition for my removal from the pulpit.

I did not preach often on this subject but often enough that the boards of the church in 1969 called me to a meeting.

I knew I was in trouble. The boards told me in no uncertain terms to quit preaching about this war. I didn't know what to say. In my mind, I was thinking I always tried to interpret the teachings of Jesus and the New Testament as they related to our lives and the world today. I believed that killing was not in accord with how we are to live. But it was obvious that these members felt threatened by my actions. A couple of months later at one of the board meetings I got so upset at their resistance to me that I finally said, "I resign!" I didn't think about what this would mean to me or to my family or what I would do. Several minister friends wrote our Church's administrative board and said, in essence, "The freedom of the pulpit is at stake!"

This board asked me not to resign, so I stayed a few months longer until I was called to serve a church in Pennsylvania. I had suffered resentment from many and felt repercussions in my digestive system, but I went there for seven years in a kind of exile. I continued to lobby for an end to the war and went to Washington another six times in peaceful marches and to lobby. Eventually through Walter Cronkite and TV footage, the shooting of Kent State students during a protest, the My Lai massacre, and *Life* magazine's gallery-like pictures of U.S. soldiers killed in a typical month, most Americans were ready to stop the war and to end its tragic consequences.

I didn't ask for, expect, or seek this experience, its pain and the discoveries I made about myself and others. I probably could have done it differently, but I didn't know how. I just felt called to speak out for what I knew was right. And I did. No regrets. •

For What I Knew Was Right

Bill Gramley is a retired Moravian minister, pastel artist, and athlete. He participates in Senior Games (writing, arts, sports) and Masters track where he holds several national records in the discus, hammer, and weight throws. Years ago he wrote *Poetic Expressions of Grief* and more recently has written three versions of *Devotional Expressions and Prayers* through the Music and Arts Ministry at Centenary United Methodist Church. Bill and his wife, Sandra, live in Lewisville, North Carolina.

An Improbable Prairie Surprise
by Calvin Vaughn

Our plan was to discover sights unknown. My 12-year-old great-niece Addyson, my best friend, Sophia, and I made up our travel trio. We launched our excursion with a flight from North Carolina to Minneapolis.

As a typical tween, Addyson's idea of adventure included shopping at the Mall of America, the country's largest shopping complex. Darting in and out of stores looking for the perfect purchase thrilled her. Her eagerness matched the "forty-niners" discovering California gold. She was excited; I was less enthusiastic. After escaping the lure and the luxury of retail life, we rented a car and began our trek through the Midwest. Our leisurely pace allowed time for adventure. We were headed nowhere and thus prepared to go anywhere.

For the next nine days we explored historical sites and places of natural wonder. Local culture awed us—at least the adults were in wonder. We made numerous stops. We paused for photos. Addyson's boredom seemed to grow. At some places, she asked to stay in the car closely holding her earbuds as if they were prized jewels. For much of the trip, she remained isolated in her own world, slumped in the back seat. She appeared unaware of the stunning landscape surrounding us.

"Look!" I yelped. "Look, look, at the gorgeous lake," I continued. Sophia turned with whispered admiration, "It is beautiful." Addyson rolled her eyes and pretended not to look. Her typical, tepid reaction from the back contrasted with the wonderment displayed from the front of the car as we forged ahead surrounded by natural artistry. But something was about to change.

We adults gawked as we journeyed through the Black Hills. Even Addyson lifted her head, holding one earbud a few inches from her ear as if she might be mildly interested. Her dark brown eyes widened. This was becoming a more exciting discovery and with an interesting surprise.

Driving through the strikingly beautiful Badlands National Park, we passed herds of bighorn sheep. When we stopped, to my astonishment, Addyson got out of the car to survey from a distance their curled horns as the grayish brown rams and ewes placed their hooves perfectly on the edges of the small rock clefts. After an extended viewing of these graceful animals, we continued down a dusty dirt road which soon began to narrow. It was there, we first saw the sign: "Prairie Dog Town Ahead." We followed. Addyson's earbuds were nowhere in sight. She sat close to the window peering into the boundless dry terrain. I strained to see the next sign and continued following, hoping for any clue that would lead us to the "town."

As we traveled along the shrinking road, my mind filled with images of historic prairie homes, important buildings, old stores, and maybe a museum showing how people once lived on the prairie. I shared my expectations. Addyson then seemed less thrilled. She lay down again in the back seat plugging her ears with her faithful companions—the earbuds.

The road narrowed; my anticipation heightened. Turning through the next curve I saw it; I eased on the brake and slowly came to a stop. Addyson raised from her slumped position while pulling the earbuds from her ears.

Before us was a weather-worn information board with faded papers. It appeared nothing else was there to see. I gazed beyond the board looking at what seemed to be endless prairie. My eyes scanned the vast open land. It was fascinating. Thousands of acres, hundreds of mounds and craters, with hundreds of adorable, chubby, little, furry, brown mammals scampering and popping up to scurry across the prairie then disappearing in and out of the tunnels.

Prairie Dog Town. My disillusioned expectation turned into a delightful surprise for us all, even the uninterested tween. We each wore huge smiles as our excitement swelled. With wide eyes, Addyson flung open the door, gave a shriek, and ran toward the prairie dogs. They perched on the mounds as if standing on an observation deck. As she approached, they darted into holes. The black-tailed mammals were only about a foot tall but fast as lightening. They were romping everywhere. Addyson was surrounded by these creatures, which dared not get close. She slowly knelt near a crater and froze in position. One peered out. Slowly he approached. Gradually Addyson

An Improbable Prairie Surprise

gently extended a hand. To our surprise, he gingerly came to her. Sniffing her hand, they explored each other. To this day, we recall that adventure with laughter and giant smiles.

Adventurous vacations, as with life, hold varying expectations. Surprising discoveries can be breathtaking for any age. I encourage everyone to travel. Go someplace new and explore. Exploration creates adventure. Adventure gives birth to discovery. Discovery presents amazing surprises. And, surprises fill our lives with joy and laughter. •

Calvin B. Vaughn, Jr. lives in Mount Airy, North Carolina, where he is retired. He has been writing for his own pleasure for 40 years. Several pieces have appeared in a local newspaper, senior aging publications and a state magazine. Currently, he is writing a collection of inspirational vignettes under the title *Life on MAin*, true stories about amazing characters in small town America.

"Luke Skywalker" and the Drain Pipe
by Vicki Easterly

T hank goodness it wasn't raining that July day, but it was hot and hard to breathe – even if you weren't a small boy stuck in a drain pipe.

Six-year-old Chris and his 4-year-old cousin JoJo were out in the farm yard picking dandelions and digging with sticks for earth worms to drop into pickle jars.

Papaw and I were sitting at his table in the cool kitchen of his little farm house, enjoying our coffee and apple delight. Through the screen door, we watched the kids picking and digging contentedly.

Papaw was a wit and had engaged me in a story of how he had once played a practical joke on his neighbor, Crow Brawner. One year they had a "biggest tomato" contest, he began. The season was nearly over, and Papaw's tomatoes were a little scrawny. Rather than admit defeat, he went to the Farmer's Market and bought a basket of the vendor's roundest, most gigantic tomatoes. All night he stayed up, tying his bought tomatoes onto his tomato stalks. Those tomatoes shone red and plump on the vine the next morning. When Crow ambled over, he good-naturedly conceded. He knew when he was beat. Reaching down to pluck one of the delicious tomatoes from the vine, Crow discovered the hidden green string that held it on. "Why, Russ Waits, you scoundrel, you should . . .

BAM! Interrupting Papaw's story, JoJo burst frantically through the door, ripping the screen all the way out. "Papaw! Auntie! Chris is caught in the drain pipe!" she yelled, almost out of breath. So engrossed were Papaw and I in his storytelling that we had taken our eyes off the kids. It couldn't have taken more than 10 seconds for those little scamps to shinny over the fence at the end of the yard where the drain pipe lay.

Up we jumped, full of fear and adrenaline, Papaw scooting along behind as fast as his 67-year-old legs would carry him. How could my little boy have found the drain pipe under the driveway, where torrents of water gush through in a rain storm? What would we find when got to the drain pipe? What if my little boy had suffocated? Yet when we got there, we found him just a little sweaty, a little dirty, but very much alive—and not at all as afraid as we were.

He was lying on his stomach in the bottom of the pipe, his right leg wedged straight up at the knee. The bottom of his foot was not budging from the top of his concrete prison. Unflustered at this predicament, he played, waging battles between his Darth Vader and Han Solo figures, which kept him company inside the giant cylinder he had dubbed his Imperial AT-AT, as we frantically pushed and pulled his leg.

I sent JoJo for a glass of water, a snack, and a cold rag. (A cold rag can heal anything from a bee sting to a broken heart.) We told Chris everything was all right, only it wasn't. It had now been one hour.

We tried mightily to dislodge his little sneakered foot from the Titan grip of that circle, but his foot would not move. By then, I was in a panic, sobbing and offering up prayers of petition. In my confounded condition, I might have murmured about calling the Bald Knob Fire Department to come out, put Chris to sleep, break the pipe, and drag him out.

Even usually unflappable Papaw, a decorated World War II veteran, announced, "Well, I thought I'd seen everything, but I ain't never seen nothing like this!" The fear in his eyes betrayed his stoicism. It had now been two hours.

Chris was still having fun, slobbering and slinging his miniature light sabers. Still imagining it all to be a great adventure, he shouted from his hollow brig. "May the force be with you!" And amazingly it was! With one last jiggle and one last mighty yank, Papaw freed my little Star Wars character from living the rest of his natural life in the drainpipe.

Except for a skinned knee, Chris was none the worse for his ordeal. I, however, was still sobbing, and now offering up prayers of thanksgiving. "Why are you crying, Mommy?" asked my extricated offspring. "Because I'm happy," I sniffled, as I hugged him too tight and walked with him back to the house.

Taking advantage of my fragile emotional state, he mustered

the courage to ask, "Can I have a Coke?"

"Anything you want, 'Luke Skywalker,' anything you want."

JoJo spent the rest of the day proudly proclaiming, "I saved Chris today! I saved Chris today!"

"Yes, you sure did!" I bragged. "Thank goodness you saved Chris today."

And thank goodness it wasn't raining. •

Vicki Easterly lives in Frankfort, Kentucky, where she is a member of the Capital City Roundtable writers' group. She has been writing for pleasure since high school. Her short story, "Hallie Holcomb's Hollow," has been published by Carnegie Press. She was selected and appeared with her first book, *Miracles in the Mundane*, at the 2018 Kentucky Book Fair. Her story, "Aunt Jessie," appeared in the 2018 Personal Essay Publishing Project, *Bearing Up*.

Silas Dooley and the Indian Brave
by William Hildebolt

The western Ohio frontier in 1805 was blessed with numerous sweet flowing springs. One such stream called Paint Creek flowed through Silas Dooley's land grant. The relationship between the arriving white settlers and the native Indians remaining in the area was delicate, at best. Removed only 10 miles east of the Indiana border (which was Indian territory in 1805), Indians were still prevalent in the surrounding countryside. Some were friendly while others were hostile. A confederation of tribes—Chippewa, Ottawa, Pottawatomi, Shawnee, Delaware, Miami, and Wyandotte—had fought alongside British units in the early 1790s when control of what the victorious United States later called the Old Northwest Territory was still contested. These native people resented white settlers intruding into their nations and laying claim to their rich, unspoiled land. Their homeland was covered primarily in forests filled with bountiful wild game.

It was a hot midsummer day, as Silas labored to clear his heavily forested land. The sun beat down relentlessly on his strong shoulders as he swung his axe and sweat dripped off his brow, stinging his eyes. He took cool relief in the spring water that flowed freely next to his three-sided lean-to. He had built this simple structure to live in as he worked relentlessly to clear his land to plant crops next spring. No other priority mattered more than getting the land cleared to become self-sufficient in growing his own food.

Silas had been at this task for several months and was making steady but slow progress. He was a single man with an axe working against huge trees and dense underbrush. As Silas was struggling with an especially difficult stump, he noticed out of the corner of his eye an Indian brave approaching. Silas eyed the man cautiously. His contact with the local Indians had been infrequent but friendly so far. But Silas also remembered from his early days growing up in Kentucky the tales of Indian raids and massacres. The Indian continued to approach and then stopped. He made hand gestures for Silas to follow him. Silas was puzzled and not too sure how to respond. He did not want to seem unfriendly; his intention was to get along with his neighboring Indians and not to insult them. But he was also fearful this could be a trap because the Indian gestured for him to put down his axe and to follow him into the woods. Other Indians could be hiding in the woods ready to ambush him. With curiosity overtaking concern, Silas reluctantly put his fears aside along with his axe. He followed the brave.

The Indian took Silas on a path across the creek and into the woods where after a short hike they came upon a freshly killed deer. The carcass had already been cut into quarters, and Silas was offered the rear haunch. He readily accepted this magnificent gift. It was the middle of summer and fresh meat was scarce. Without refrigeration or salting, meat spoiled in a matter of days. This deer represented the first meat that Silas had eaten in many weeks.

The brave grabbed one of the front quarters, placed it on his shoulder and took the lead back towards Silas's camp. As they retraced their steps, Silas noticed that the Indian was deviating from their original path. He did not think too much about why they were taking a detour other than maybe it was a shorter track. The underbrush was thick, and it was difficult to see ahead and to keep pace with the Indian. Suddenly came a loud thud and then a snapping and breaking of twigs and limbs. The Indian set out on a dead run. A few steps later, Silas saw the brave disappear into the dark forest as he was surrounded immediately by an angry swarm of stinging hornets!

Silas knew instantly why the brave had purposely changed course. He wanted to walk past the hornets' nest and to hit it with the leg of the deer. Hornets have a powerful sting but not strong enough to dislodge that hind quarter from Silas's shoulder. He raced toward Paint Creek and jumped in headlong still holding onto his precious dinner!

Despite the hornets and Indians playing practical jokes on him, Silas went on to clear his land and to build a log cabin. Silas Dooley became a successful farmer in western Ohio and indeed a loving father and grandfather. In 1830, he built the house in which I grew up. •

Silas Dooley and the Indian Brave

William M. Hildebolt lives in Winston-Salem, North Carolina.
He has published two non-fiction books. *The Professional Entrepreneur*
looks at the characteristics needed to succeed as an entrepreneur.
It's in There looks at the development of Prego® spaghetti sauce.
He also enjoys writing stories on the history of his family's 200 years
on an Ohio farm.

Swamp Creature

by Randell Jones

I was 20 years old when I first met Booger. He was a middle-aged crew chief for the Georgia Highway Department's Soil and Materials Laboratory in Forest Park. I was working a summer job out of Atlanta in 1970 trying to figure out why I wanted to be a Georgia Tech civil engineer since I was just about to graduate as one. As it happened, I learned a lot that summer, but not much of it was about engineering.

Booger's job as crew chief was to get his five roughnecks out the door every Monday and onto the road to some out-of-the-way, backwoods place—a place some overweight bureaucrat stuffed into an undersized short-sleeved dress shirt with a clip-on tie had decided a road needed to go. He'd done this one afternoon after lunch as he leaned over his ample stomach and nodded off for an hour-long nap. (This was 50 years ago, so apologies to all current, hard-working, state-government employees. Lester "Pickrick Drumstick" Maddox was governor then, so this is not about you.)

Our job was to drill a hole—a deep hole, eight inches in diameter and sometimes 60 feet deep. Then we'd take a sample of the soil. (That's the engineering term for what the layman calls "dirt.") Sometimes Booger's crew pulled "swamp duty," and that was my chance to empathize with the heroes who toiled to build the Panama Canal through foreboding, disease-ridden jungle, slogging their way through mosquito-infested tropical forests. They got glory. I got $2.50 an hour.

Georgia was still working to build Interstate 95 through the low-lying, paper-company timberlands around Brunswick. Testing the soil in this area took special equipment and extra effort, but the test results were always the same: black, wet muck. The weather that summer was always the same too—sunny, hot, and muggy. And if you didn't get carried away by the humidity, then the mosquitos were glad to oblige. It was said that around the swamps the mosquitoes were so big that they could stand flat-footed and goose a turkey. I never saw one do it, but you did hear lots of strange animal sounds out there in the woods, and some of that could have been turkeys surprised from behind.

We entered the swamplands from the last paved road leading from—what passed in these parts—for civilization. We were in a drill rig known as a "swamp boat." It's only source of locomotion was to wind up on its bow-mounted winch the cable that was stretched out from it and hooked around some shallow-rooted tree perhaps 100 feet away across the soup-like quagmire. As the cable spooled onto the winch, the swamp boat inched its way toward the tree with agonizing lethargy, like an overloaded 18-wheeler stuck in low gear and grinding its way up a steep incline. When the boat had slid and sloshed a sufficient distance toward its target tree, another tree was selected and the poor, unfortunate low man on the totem pole—yours truly—would slog through knee-deep muck with block and tackle slung over my shoulders hauling the cable out from the winch as I fought to keep my balance and my sense of humor.

After a long morning of maneuvering this sled in the sludge, we set about preparing to drill some test holes. And though we were surrounded by a swamp for miles around we had to search a good bit to find a pool from which to pump a sufficient supply of drilling water back to the swamp boat. That search was mine by default, not choice. So, I set out from the drill rig with 40 pounds of pump clutched between my forearms and a coil of hydraulic hose trailing behind me as I sank deeper into the mud. With each step, I made an unmistakable suction-breaking "th-thock" when I pulled my foot knee-high to free it from the muck.

That's how I came to fall—backwards mind you—flat on my back with a heavy pump pushing on my chest as the swamp began to absorb me. The muck oozed upward slowly over my ears and encircled my face like a nun's habit before I was able to extricate myself from the slime and get back on my feet. Surprised and embarrassed, my animated facial expressions and my excited string of expletives contrasted starkly with the dull, grayish-brown mud that now colored my backside . . . and my mood.

But it was all in a day's work, a dirty day but a day, nonetheless. Fortunately, there were only five of them that week, and then I'd be off on another assignment with another crew.

Thank goodness! What could be worse than this? •

(Continued in "Jimmy, Poison Ivy, and a Tattooed Moon")

Copyright 2019, Randell Jones

Randell Jones lives in Winston-Salem, North Carolina. He is the author of several award-winning history books, including *In the Footsteps of Daniel Boone*, and two videos. Since 2007, he has served as an invited member of the Road Scholars Speakers Bureau of the North Carolina Humanities Council. He writes, speaks, and publishes as Daniel Boone Footsteps at www.DanielBooneFootsteps.com (also www.RandellJones.com). He published *Bearing Up*, a companion anthology to *Exploring*, in 2018.

Jimmy, Poison Ivy, and a Tattooed Moon
by Randell Jones

H oot was a ruddy-complexioned, barrel-chested good ol' boy who wore his jeans real tight and fastened them down low underneath his stomach, giving him that seven-months pregnant look that women just adored. He had tattoos on his arms and ran a pretty tight ship as supervisor of a soil-testing crew for the Georgia Highway Department. "Tight ship" was a term Hoot had grown to respect because of his time in the Navy starting at age 17; and, as he approached his mid-30s, he still thought he was a teenager. Jerry Jeff Walker must have had Hoot in mind in his country song: "He's 34 and drinkin' in some honky tonk, just kickin' hippies' asses and raisin' hell."

South Georgia summers in the flat coastal plain stretching down to Savannah can reach 100° by noon. One such day in summer 1970, Hoot's crew was drilling through some ground-cover and recirculating the wash water which was bringing the soil shavings back to the surface. I was the rod slinger, a student working a summer job. A gasket in the drill head was leaking and spraying me with that cool, muddy wash water that had just come back up from 40 feet down in the dark earth where everything is 55° year-round. It felt so good in the blistering heat.

That night I sensed a tingling all over. By the weekend, my legs were so red and swollen I couldn't bend them. That ground-cover was poison ivy, and the wash water had picked up the irritating oil from the root system. I had oozing, poison ivy blisters covering 60% of my body. My chest, my arms, every-thing was enflamed. All I could do for four days was lie in bed mentally numb from the stupefying itch and try not to scratch. But once a day I would take a shower in near-scalding-hot water that would send a rush shivering through my whole body. It was nearly heaven for 15 seconds. But like a lot of life's experiences, the momentary pleasure was hardly worth the suffering.

When we finished each day's work, the crew checked into a motel to shower for dinner. We shared rooms, of course—state travel rules. One evening I was waiting on the shower when Hoot popped through the door from the adjoining room in his underwear. He spun around, dropped his shorts, and shot me a moon. And right there, staring back at me, were these two eyes—tattooed, one on each cheek of his butt—and in an arc above them were the tattooed words: "I've got my eyes on you." That was the day I realized what a deeply religious man Hoot was, because nobody but God's Own Drunk could get smashed enough to get a tattoo like that.

At long last the summer passed, and from it all I learned more about making a life than making a living. But my labors did not go unrewarded. In January 1971, I got a phone call from one of the civil engineering professors at Georgia Tech telling me that I had been awarded the Radnor J. Paquette Award as the Outstanding Student on the Job-Training Program for the Georgia Highway Department. Lordy, Lordy. There I was with three-plus years of rigorous engineering education under my belt at one of the most prestigious technical colleges in the country and I was getting an award for digging good post-holes. I guess we sometimes miss recognizing our own best talents until others point them out to us. I was pleased to be good at something.

I was to receive an engraved watch at the annual dinner of the Georgia Highway Contractors Association, a prestigious gathering of the Who's Who of official Georgia "highway-dom." I sat at the head table on the dais, looking over a sea of flat-tops and leisure suits. I sported a scraggly beard with hair draped over my ears. My appearance, no doubt, signaled to all that I was an alien from another planet whose presence there was for the amusement of a universal intelligence with a warped sense of humor.

They gave me the watch anyway, engraved "Kenneth R. Jones" (whoever that was). The recently inaugurated governor of Georgia, who had sat only a few feet away during the dinner and who was himself a former student at Georgia Tech, stood to congratulate me and to shake my hand as he gave me a big toothy grin. I was meeting Jimmy Carter and shook the hand of the man who would go on to become President of United

Jimmy, Poison Ivy, and a Tattooed Moon

States, a job he thought he wanted but probably didn't understand enough to know if he did or not until he got it and then
it was too late. That much we had in common. •

(Kenneth) Randell Jones lives in Winston-Salem, North Carolina. He
is the author of several award-winning history books, including *In the
Footsteps of Daniel Boone*, and two videos. Since 2007, he has served as
an invited member of the Road Scholars Speakers Bureau of the
North Carolina Humanities Council. He writes, speaks, and publishes as Daniel Boone Footsteps at www.DanielBooneFootsteps.com
(also www.RandellJones.com). He published *Bearing Up*, a companion
anthology to *Exploring*, in 2018.

CPSIA information can be obtained
at www.ICGtesting.com
Printed in the USA
FSHW011248140721
83104FS